50 RACES
TO RUN
BEFORE
YOU DIE

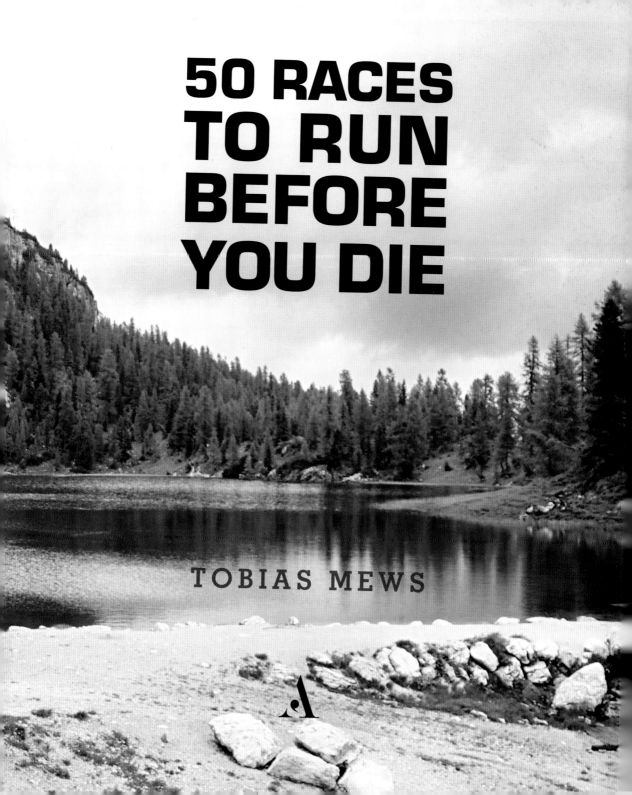

50 RACES TO RUN BEFORE YOU DIE

TOBIAS MEWS

Quarto is the authority on a wide range of topics.
Quarto educates, entertains and enriches the lives of
our readers – enthusiasts and lovers of hands-on living.
www.QuartoKnows.com

First published in Great Britain
2016 by Aurum Press Ltd
74–77 White Lion Street
Islington
London N1 9PF
www.aurumpress.co.uk

A catalogue record for this book is available from the British Library.

ISBN 978 1 78131 444 9

10 9 8 7 6 5 4 3 2 1
2020 2019 2018 2017 2016

Typeset in 8.5/12.5pt Caecilia by carrdesignstudio.com
Printed in China

For my mother,
Anna Clemence Mews

CONTENTS

LEFT TOP TO BOTTOM: Tough Mudder, Marathon du Medoc, Transalpine Run

FOREWORD

For me, the thrill of racing is surpassed by that feeling of adrenalin at the start. Knowing that your mind is going to ask your body tough questions it will try to avoid answering, but ultimately your success and enjoyment will be determined by how well you answer those questions.

Will you reach the finish line? How fast will you be? Have you reached new limits? And the rush of endorphins and adrenaline when you pass through the tape knowing you have given your all.

Competition has always been a large part of my life. But my proudest moment in sport was not crossing the line at the Sydney or Athens Olympics but lying in a quarantine room on the day of the Opening Ceremony at the 1996 Atlanta Olympics. After four years of training I contracted tonsillitis and was pulled out of racing on the day the Games started. Lying in that quarantine room/broom cupboard it would have been easier to have quit and got a job because there was no guarantee that the same thing wouldn't happen in four years time. But I decided that I wasn't going to end my Olympic career not having made the start line.

Making that decision under those circumstances and having experienced those lows made me a stronger athlete at the Sydney Olympics four years later. That, as well as training with, and hanging off the coattails of Sir Steve Redgrave and Sir Matthew Pinsent.

The Marathon des Sables.

Since retiring from rowing I have enjoyed the opportunity to test myself on some of the most challenging of endurance races, including crossing America, facing down the heat and sands of the Sahara Desert at the Marathon de Sables, rowing across the Atlantic and racing to the South Pole. Whether it's as part of a team or as an individual the common theme has been to learn a new skill, experience new surroundings, push my mind and body to the limit. But more importantly being a small speck in a massive environment is totally different to the often sterile world of sport.

Running is arguably the most pure, natural, time-efficient sport and can be done in virtually any location. No matter how experienced you are or how much training you have done, you can still go out there and run. With all the time we now spend at computers and desks, it's the best way to get away and zone out.

In *50 Races to Run Before You Die*, Tobias has brought together some of the world's best races. Those that get you out of bed on a Saturday morning (despite your partner thinking you're weird) and into your local park, to races that encourage you to dream big and test yourself, or even provide a very worthwhile excuse to visit the Cayman Islands. Whether its the muddy obstacle courses that are all about fun, to the heights of England's fells with trail runs that open you up to the beauty to be found here in England's hills, these races are iconic as much for their challenges as for their locations.

I suffered from horrendous ulcerated blisters when I was racing to the South Pole, partly due to the extreme conditions but mostly due to me making the wrong decisions at the crucial time. I was getting my feet treated by a doctor at the South Pole when a bloke stuck his head into the tent and sympathetically said 'you think those are blisters you should do the Marathon des Sables!' I signed up as soon as I got back to the UK. The chance to prove I could make the right decision at the right time in a competitive situation would mean I'd learned my lessons from Antarctica. The fact that I finished the highest place a Brit had achieved in the race's 25 year history showed that I made the right decisions.

Whichever run you pick to start you off and whatever your goal for running, I can assure you that when you are amongst the runners in a pack hearing the crowds applaud you on, or experiencing the quiet moments on a open stretch of track in the face of a new challenge, you might just find you surprise yourself. And with this selection of epic races, you might just want to run them all.

James Cracknell

INTRODUCTION

As I write up the final race in this book, recalling my last 200-mile journey across the mountainous spine of Wales, I look downwards towards my feet. My ankles have been consumed by my calves, my swollen feet make my flip-flops look as if I'm wearing a thong, skin is missing in between some of my toes and at least one nail might soon be lost but none of these things matter, because the satisfaction of finishing the Dragon's Back Race (page 232) is worth every ounce of discomfort. It is an iconic race steeped in history and legend and for me, one of the best races to 'run before you die'.

Over the course of the past 10 years, I've raced across five continents and a dozen countries. I've run through deserts and jungles, across islands and mountain ranges, along coastlines, through forests, woods, cities and villages. After a moment of procrastination, I've worked out that in order to 'research' the 50 races in this book I've raced over 2,700 miles and climbed (and descended) over 116,000 metres. That's the equivalent of 13 times up and down Mount Everest, and 10 miles beyond the edge of outer space. The figures make me want to sit down, have a stiff drink and book a massage.

I long ago realised I'd never be good enough to become a professional athlete. Having only started running 'seriously' at the age of 31, I was a bit behind the learning curve. But what I did possess was curiosity and a willingness to explore what I was capable of. Indeed, the endorphins of finishing a race were so great, all the pain that I'd experienced was erased. And if I had said, 'never again' at the end of a race, before I knew it, I was researching my next one: it's addictive.

For me, running and racing have been a vehicle to a whole new world. They've allowed me to see places that I'd only ever dreamt of, and pushed the boundaries of my self-imposed limitations, making me stronger, healthier and fitter. And it's also thanks to running that I met my wife Zayne, who's run many of the races with me – not just as my 'wife' in The UK Wife Carrying Race (page 48).

Running has been a journey. I've not plunged straight into hard as nails races that claim to be the 'toughest in the world', but begun with those in which I know I can complete. And as my confidence built, I looked for bigger challenges, ones that would take me further, higher and faster.

Destination Races are by far my favourite type. These are the ones located in stunning locations you'd want to visit whether you were racing or not. Which means they're also perfect for bringing your family along, from exploring the Yorkshire Dales in the Three Peaks Race (page 198) to the towering Dolomites in the Lavaredo Ultra Trail (page 182). And the beauty is, by entering a race most of the logistics are taken care of. All you have to do is run.

I've included marathons, tower running, sky running, ultra-running, multi-stage races, wife carrying, one-milers, 5Ks, 10Ks, zombie racing, fell running, trail running, swim running, 24-hour relay races, obstacle-course races, mountain marathons and so much more. Where possible, I've included statistics on the cut-offs, the winner's time, location, website and various other bits of information you need to take part. And for transparency's sake, I've also included my own finishing time – something for the competitive amongst you to beat. There is literally a race for every occasion and every level of fitness. Which is why I've split the book up into three volumes:

Good for Beginners: More focused on fun than slogging it out, no experience necessary.

Sucker for Punishment: New terrains and new challenges. For some of these races you need to have marathon experience.

Hard as Nails: Grit, stamina, and essential experience required.

Not everyone is competitive. For some the journey is more important than a time or position, but no matter who you are, there is no greater way to get an endorphin fix than finishing a race. So get out there and sign up for a race. Once you get started, there's no turning back!

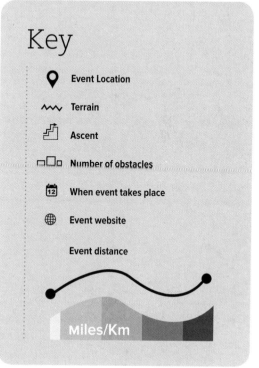

Key

⬤ Event Location

〜 Terrain

⌁ Ascent

▫▢▫ Number of obstacles

📅 When event takes place

🌐 Event website

Event distance

Miles/Km

GOOD FOR BEGINNERS

TOUGH MUDDER

UK and worldwide

20+

 Muddy obstacle course; high likelihood of water feature

All year round

www.toughmudder.co.uk

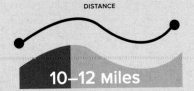

DISTANCE

10–12 Miles

HR MIN SEC
0 1 3 4 0 0

TOBIAS' FINISHING TIME

78% COMPLETION RATE

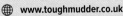

'Don't worry, mate, I've got you, should you fall!' shouted the diver treading water in the cold and murky depths several metres below me. On any other occasion those words would be reassuring, but since I was in the precarious position of being caught between a rock and a hard place, this did little to calm my nerves. You see, I'd got myself into a bit of a pickle on the monkey bar obstacle of the UK's inaugural Tough Mudder race.

Eager to prove my worth by crossing the 20m long beast – and also to reassure myself that my army skills hadn't abandoned me – I'd stubbornly carried on swinging away to the point of exhaustion. And now, I was stuck. If I dropped from where I was, one leg would touch the platform, the other would be in the water. It didn't bear thinking about. However, if I tried to swing across to the two remaining bars, I might succeed but there was also a strong likelihood that I wouldn't. Suffice to say, it didn't quite go according to plan and I was nursing a sore groin for a couple of days.

I don't think I'd be wrong in saying Tough Mudder is the biggest name in obstacle course racing. Founded by two Brits, Guy Livingstone and Will Dean, they have created a tribe and a movement, or as Will puts it in one of their videos: 'We're getting people back to basics … And the teamwork and the camaraderie part, that's what we're all about.' To date, well over 1.5 million people have taken part in a Tough Mudder event, and bearing in mind that in 2015, they had more than 50 global events, that number is set to grow.

What sets Tough Mudder apart from many of the other obstacle course races is that it's not a race 'but a challenge', and when you enter, you must take the pledge that you'll put 'teamwork and camaraderie before your course time' and 'help your fellow mudders complete the course'. There is no real winning time as it's not a race; therefore no timing chips, or indeed winners.

You don't have to have a six-pack or guns the size of Arnold Schwarzenegger to do a

Tough Mudder is as much about team work as having a good time.

Top tips

- Enter as a team – it's a lot more fun
- Wear clothes that you don't mind trashing
- Train your upper body – you'll need it for the monkey bars!

Tough Mudder event, although many mudders do. Nor do you have to go bare-chested (which must come as a relief to the women entrants!), but you do have to go there with a smile and say to yourself, 'Today is all about having fun.'

Tough Mudder is essentially a 'team event' and I well remember my first race, which I tackled alone. I had to jump over a wall just to get into the starting pen of one of the earlier waves and I cringed with a mixture of apprehension and embarrassment as a man with a megaphone shouted out the aforementioned Tough Mudder Pledge, which we all had to repeat. My apprehension lay in worrying that I might need help to get over the obstacles on my own, but if you possess a modicum of fitness and strength then you can do most of them, except perhaps for the Pyramid Scheme, where you really do need teammates to build the pyramid.

However, times have changed since my inaugural outing in 2012. Tough Mudder has just got a whole lot tougher, to the point where you're almost in the *Crystal Maze* of obstacle courses. Indeed, every year the organisers bring out new obstacles that will have you scratching your head, provoke a sharp intake of breath or cause you to wipe mud from your face, but never your grin. With names such as the Ring of Fire, Dirty Ballerina, the King of Swingers, Electroshock Therapy and Funky Monkey, you know you're in for a good time.

Once you've lost your Tough Mudder virginity, you have the option, upon completing the 'Legionnaires' Loop', of joining the Mudder Legion – the official community of multi-mudders. And every time you sign up for another event, you'll receive a different coloured headband according to the number of events completed, from green for two Mudders to black for those who've done ten or more. You'll also get an exclusive obstacle and the option of bypassing the Electroshock Therapy – it's not all bad! And if that's not enough to keep your interest sustained, then you might want to try the World's Toughest Mudder, where you'll do as many 10-mile loops as possible within 24 hours. Tempted?

2 BUPA WESTMINSTER MILE

London, UK | 〰〰 **Road** | 📅 **May** | 🌐 www.bupawestminstermile.co.uk

DISTANCE

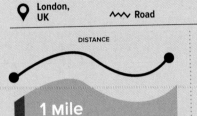

1 Mile

HR MIN SEC
0 0 0 4 3 1
FASTEST TIME (KNOWN)

0 0 0 5 0 8
TOBIAS' FINISHING TIME

99% COMPLETION RATE

Before marathons came along, there was only one distance that really mattered – the Mile – a distance widely acknowledged to be the perfect combination of speed and endurance. It is the ultimate test.

From an athlete's point of view, the Mile is considered 'middle distance'. But if you were to ask someone how far the English statute mile is, almost certainly they wouldn't be able to tell you. The answer is 1,760 yards, the distance as defined by the Weights and Measures Act of Parliament in 1593. For years people battled it out, walking and running, professionals and amateurs alike, often as a wager for gamblers and spectators to see how fast they could cover the Mile. But it wasn't until 1953 that the 4-Minute Mile was broken, when Roger Bannister, with the help of pacemakers Chris Brasher and Chris Chataway, famously ran 3:59:4 at Iffley Road Track in Oxford.

Nowadays, the British Mile has fallen to the metric mile of 1,500m – but the original still lives on. And there's no better way to test your metal than at the Bupa Westminster Mile on

arguably Britain's most famous road, The Mall in London SW1.

Although I had run countless marathons and ultra-marathons (any race longer than the classic marathon distance of 26.2 miles), I'd never run just one measly mile on its own. In fact, I didn't even know how to pace myself. Do you go flat out as fast as you can go? Or do you hold back and kick in, in the second half?

The previous month, in 2014, Kenya's Wilson Kipsang broke the marathon world record at London, averaging an astonishing 4:45 min/mile. I figured if he could do that for 26 miles, I should be able to do it for one. Wishful thinking.

Each participant is allocated a wave based upon their predicted time. Join the first wave at your peril.

Top tips

- Do a decent warm-up beforehand with mobilisation exercises to lower the risk of injury
- Don't go flat out in the first 200m as you'll need to keep something in the tank

Despite being May, the weather was not kind to us. Wind and rain threatened to turn this into a short and very wet race. As I approached the start line, I noticed lots of people limbering up, doing short sprints up and down The Mall, along with various mobilisation exercises such as leg swings and acceleration runs. Of course in this race there wouldn't be time to 'warm up' once it started: either it happened now, or in the bath at home later that day.

As I followed suit and limbered up, I remembered the wise words of former World Champion and Olympic silver medallist Steve Cram: 'It's important to warm up properly before the Mile. When the gun goes, run hard but not so hard that by 200m you're unable to maintain your pace.' Hah, easier said than done!

Usually I would join the front of the start line, confident of being able to hold my own. But on this occasion I felt shy, as though being an ultra-runner, I didn't belong there. The gun went off and I jostled into place amongst a melee of legs and elbows, as everyone fought for position on our way towards Admiralty Arch. My head was saying, 'Hold something back, don't go too fast early on,' whilst my body was trying to keep track of my cadence.

All of a sudden, when I found myself behind a wall of fellow runners and with no room to overtake them, I regretted not pushing further towards the front. As we turned the corner on to Horse Guards Road, I tried to find a space in which to overtake, but I wasn't having any luck.

Passing Horse Guards Parade on our left, before I knew it we were making another turn on to Birdcage Walk. The previous month I had been running along this very stretch in the final mile of the London Marathon. Now I was seeing a sign reading '800m to go' – a distance that I had to remind myself was actually halfway.

I found a space amongst the cohort of runners and tried to pick things up a notch, whilst remembering the second part of Steve's advice: 'The mile is undoubtedly a short race but it's long enough that if you go out too hard, the last half will be very difficult.' Luckily, I'd accidentally obeyed his advice and found enough puff to keep my pace up, passing Wellington Barracks in a blur before approaching the final turn onto Spur Road, where the finish line in front of Buckingham Palace awaited me.

The last sign I saw was '100m to go' with the countdown in approaching 4.50. I had it in the bag, I thought. Although I might not beat Kipsang's time, I reckoned I could still go below five minutes. But as I ran towards the finish, feeling as if my lungs could burst, I realised I was not Usain Bolt, nor could I run 100m in less than ten seconds!

I crossed the line in 5:08. The Bupa Westminster Mile might not be a long way, but I had found a new respect for this distance – and a love for this race. As I collected a rather fancy medal and made my way back to the bag drop-off and changing area, I vowed I'd be back.

The final 200m stretch along Birdcage Walk. This might not sound far, but can feel like forever when running at your anaerobic limit!

GOOD FOR BEGINNERS

3 ROYAL PARKS FOUNDATION HALF MARATHON

London's Royal Parks, UK   Road   📅 October   🌐 www.royalparkshalf.com

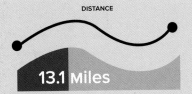

DISTANCE

13.1 Miles

	HR	MIN	SEC
	0 1	0 5	4 0

FASTEST TIME (KNOWN)

| | 0 1 | 1 9 | 3 4 |

TOBIAS' FINISHING TIME

99% COMPLETION RATE

Living in London can make you a little blasé about the 5,000 green acres that provide an oasis of calm in one of the world's biggest and busiest capital cities. Hyde Park, Green Park, St James's Park, Kensington Gardens … they're familiar names to all of us who work, play and have our homes in London. And not just familiar names – most of us have cycled or strolled through them at one time or another.

So you might be forgiven for thinking that there would be nothing special about taking part in the Royal Parks Foundation Half Marathon. But nothing could be further from the truth. In fact, there was no struggle at all to resist the alarm call on a brisk and showery Sunday morning in October, and head off for the start of the race at Hyde Park.

It's not just the aforementioned parks that you get a chance to run through – there's Westminster Bridge, which you cross without the roar of traffic in your ears and the scent of diesel in your nose. And you whizz past Buckingham Palace and the Royal Albert Hall without a car in sight: it's London as you've never seen it before. Due to road closures, the course can alter subtly from year to year. But one thing is certain: it's always 13.1 miles!

For the past seven years, since this spectacular half marathon was created in 2008, it has raised over £320 million for more than 500 UK charities and established itself as one of the premier fundraising half marathons in the UK, if not Europe. In fact, it's still the only one of its kind where you have the opportunity to run by – and through – the landmarks of a capital city.

By 8.45 a.m. – 15 minutes before the start, some 12,000 runners (the number has grown to 16,000 since 2011) were assembled at the starting point in Hyde Park and the atmosphere was amazing, the lively music giving runners every encouragement to limber up. And of course, since this is a race run by many for good causes, it wasn't just Lycra on display, but the odd dragon and squirrel making an appearance too.

I decided this was a race to enjoy, rather than simply to 'beast' myself. So I set off thoughtfully and at a gentler pace than my usual frenetic approach. This is not a race that is suddenly going to force you into umpteen metres of ascent and descent. The start at Hyde Park is flat and this decidedly 'unhilly' course through the capital extends for the full 13.1 miles. But

Runners making the turn on Westminster Bridge, with the Houses of Parliament in the background.

don't be deceived: *flat* may be a bonus but there's something about running on roads, no matter how beautiful the scenery, that still makes your feet throb and your hamstrings twitch.

As we came to the halfway point, near to the Serpentine, I began to up my pace. The crowds along the route were urging us on and I felt the need to push myself harder. A light breeze was starting up, leaves were falling heavily across the tarmac, but in keeping with the green spirit of this race, not the slightest glimpse of discarded plastic bottles, leaflets or cartons could be seen. This is a race that follows a 'no waste' philosophy, from sustainably made T-shirts to recycled polyester.

As I swung around the final corner on to South Carriage Drive, the Royal Albert Hall standing proud to my right, I caught a glimpse of the finish line, just 500m ahead, giving me the impetus for a final energetic spurt.

The oak-leaf finisher's medal is made of wood in true keeping with the ecological spirit of the race. I couldn't help but feel a sense of pride as it was hung around my neck – not just for achieving a reasonable finish but doing so in the city of London itself.

Top tips

- Familiarise yourself with the course as it can subtly change from year to year
- Check out the activity zone at the finish line – it's great fun!

BELOW: The course takes you past many of London's iconic landmarks, including Buckingham Palace.

OPPOSITE: The route takes runners along The Mall towards Buckingham Palace, before returning to Hyde Park.

4

GOOD FOR BEGINNERS
HELLRUNNER

Longmoor Camp,
Hampshire, UK   Trail, sand and bog   12 January   www.hellrunner.co.uk

DISTANCE

8–10 Miles

HR	MIN	SEC

FASTEST TIME (KNOWN)

TOBIAS' FINISHING TIME

98%
COMPLETION
RATE

On the basis that I've completed the HellRunner
five times in a row, one might say I'm either
a sucker for punishment or looking for
redemption. Perhaps it's a bit of both, bearing
in mind that I'm a fully signed-up member of
their 'Nutter's Club – Wall of Pain' for those
who've completed five or more of these races.
But regardless of how you like to spend your
weekend, you know you're in for a treat when
a race calls on the Devil as its business partner
and boasts natural obstacles such as the Bogs
of Doom and the Hills of Hell. And of course,
where better to find a 'hellish' 8–10 mile course
than the Army training ground of Longmoor
Camp in Liss, Hampshire? Bogs, sandy hills,
small lakes, rutted trails, tough climbs and
treacherous descents … it has it all.

On the first occasion I did this race, I was still
in the Army. I'd run with heavy backpacks up
and down its stony paths so this would surely
be a piece of cake. Oh, how I underestimated
this cross-country race, that's become one of
the most popular in the UK.

You can find HellRunners 'Up North', 'Down
South' or 'In the Chilts', but my association with
this wonderful race, one of the original mud
races in the UK, is very much in the South. And
being an hour from London, it's not too difficult
to reach, as long as you don't mind waking up
at an ungodly hour to get there!

HellRunner has no 'obstacles' as such –
rather natural features carved out of the ground
by Army vehicles doing their stuff. But one

ABOVE: If you're vertically challenged, you may have to swim
through the Bogs of Doom.

BELOW: If you had hoped to stay dry, think again.

LEFT: The Bogs of Doom.

Top tips

- Take lots of warm kit for after the race (including a towel)
- You'll need trail shoes with a decent grip yet able to drain water

thing it does have is a lot of hills. They might not be long, but they're short, sharp and pack a punch – certainly enough to make you out of breath and your legs to course with cramp.

The start is rather fun. A man dressed as the Devil, atop a set of giant stilts, sets us off, accompanied by a haze of smoke grenades, making it virtually impossible to see where you're going. But of course, that's the whole point. Luckily the first mile or so is fast and flat and a chance to try and get some distance between you and all. But then you hit the first few hills to warm you up before a waist-height water feature cools you down – whilst ensuring your shoes are uncomfortably wet early on in the race.

As I progressed along the course in an oxygen-deprived state, it became very clear that I wasn't as fit as I'd imagined myself to be – at least not fit enough to be competitive. And then I hit the Hills of Hell. That was enough to turn me from running mode to zombie shuffle.

OPPOSITE: Sand, bog, water, gravel – there's every type of terrain you can think of.

ABOVE: Perfect training for those doing the Marathon des Sables?

But the Bogs of Doom lay in wait. You know when you're approaching them because you'll hear the squeals of laughter from the crowds and simultaneous gasps of shock from the competitors. As you finally arrive at the water's murky edge, you'll discover an enormous 20m long trench filled with the darkest, coldest, sludge-like water you can imagine. And if you're somewhat vertically challenged, like yours truly, soon you'll be up to your neck in the stuff!

Soaking wet and feeling pretty sorry for myself, I made a poor attempt at trying to run before I was once again in another giant puddle – by which point I couldn't feel anything below my neck. A very sandy section later (good preparation, I later discovered, for the Marathon des Sables, see also page 178), and the finish was then in sight. The relief of crossing the line before being sick is something I'll never forget but it didn't put me off. I returned the following four years, determined to better my time.

5 THE GRIM CHALLENGE

Various locations, UK 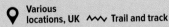 Trail and track

December

www.grimchallenge.co.uk

DISTANCE

8.1 Miles
(2014, VARIES DEPENDING ON YEAR)

HR	MIN	SEC
0 0	4 4	2 6

FASTEST TIME (KNOWN)

| 0 0 | 5 3 | 3 0 |

TOBIAS' FINISHING TIME

98% COMPLETION RATE

'I pity the poor buggers going through this first,' said the man standing next to me, whilst casually throwing a pebble onto the giant 30m long frozen puddle before us. Being December, the temperature was hovering around the freezing mark.

I watched the pebble scatter along the surface before resting somewhere in the middle. '*Crikey!*

How in the hell are we supposed to get through that?' I pondered, rubbing my shins in anticipation moments before the race was about to begin. Under normal circumstances I wouldn't be too concerned about the odd bit of ice, but having previously finished in the top ten of this race, I was well aware that as a lead runner, I'd also become something of an icebreaker.

OPPOSITE: The calm before the storm. With the Challenge taking place in winter, you'll be grateful to start running – just to warm up!

ABOVE: While fancy dress is optional, it makes it a lot more fun.

The Grim Challenge may only be eight miles long, which isn't that far in the grand scheme of things, but don't let that deceive you. The 'UK's original and best off-road series' is GRIM in name and in nature. As the organisers cheerfully note, it's just a case of 'Grim and bare it!' But some might argue differently because if it was really *that* bad, you wouldn't get 3,500 runners entering the sell-out race.

Spread over two days you can choose to enter either as an individual or as a team of three (single-sex or mixed). And having done this race twice as an individual, I'd argue it's more fun as a team, especially as it's only two weeks before Christmas and therefore a perfect opportunity to dig out the fancy dress kit.

As you might expect, this is not a race that necessarily attracts the world's finest cross-

country talent – quite possibly they've got better things to do than roll around in the mud – which is why if you've got any decent speed and endurance behind you, there's a good chance you could do quite well. But if you're looking to set a Personal Best (PB), then this is probably not the event for you.

The British Military Fitness boys are on hand to dish out a few warm-up manoeuvres to prevent you from seizing up on the start line. Nevertheless, by the time you begin the race, you're grateful to be running. Cut from Army vehicle testing tracks, the course, which changes depending on what the British Army is up to, is always guaranteed to be wet, muddy and downright hard. It is also littered with pools of water, hiding deep vehicle ruts that you'll curse as you trip over them, sending you sprawling head first into the murky depths.

Whilst the Grim Challenge doesn't call itself, nor pretend to be, an obstacle course race, more a 'mud race', it does have a few obstacles to keep you on your toes, or indeed trip you up, ranging from a tyre run to cargo nets that you must leopard crawl under. However, the real obstacles are the short and sharp inclines that drain your legs and the sometimes waist-deep, freezing-cold puddles that literally take your breath away, the highlight being the 'Big Puddle' towards the end.

OPPOSITE: Although not an obstacle course, the water features combined with camo nets are enough to put a smile on your face.

ABOVE: Cunningly placed cargo nets leave you no choice but to get wet.

Top tips

- Wear synthetic, fast-wicking (quick-drying) clothes
- Use off-road running shoes with plenty of grip
- Go through the puddles and not around them – it's more fun!

Of course, it would be easier to avoid some of the puddles, but that would take the fun out of it. After all, what's the point in doing a race with a tag line, 'Run, Wade or Crawl' if you don't actually do any of those things?

By the time I'd got to some of the larger puddles, some kind soul had broken up portions of the ice – thus causing fewer lacerations to my shins – perhaps to the disappointment of the crowds of family and friends gathered around the main water features, waiting for someone to fall in. As I rolled into the finish, soaking wet and still a bit on the chilly side, I was nevertheless grinning from ear to ear. It may not be as tough as some of the other races, but it's certainly just as much fun!

Corfe Castle,
Dorset, UK   Trail and grass   575m   12 September   www.pooleac.co.uk/the-beast

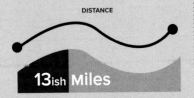

13ish Miles

DISTANCE

HR   MIN   SEC
0 1   1 9   0 0
FASTEST TIME (KNOWN)

0 2   0 1   1 7
TOBIAS' FINISHING TIME

99%
COMPLETION
RATE

It's September 2004 and I'm sitting on the ground beneath Corfe Castle, feeling a little worse for wear. 'Are you OK, Tobias?' my mother asks with concern after seeing me finish The Beast, a half marathon-ish distance race on the Dorset coast.

'I think I'm going to be sick,' I answer, pale-faced.

'Well, you could have picked a slightly easier race for your first half marathon!' she replies.

She was right. But then again, I've never been known for being sensible. Besides, when a race called The Beast takes place on your doorstep (I was on a posting with the Army), there's little excuse not to do it.

The idea behind the race was born, as are so many these days, over a few pints in the pub. That was back in 1994. Now, more than 20 years later and part of the Purbeck Trail Series, the Poole Athletic Club-organised Beast is still going strong. Thanks to coast erosion the course has changed a bit over the years, with the distance fluctuating slightly, but it's always been regarded by those who've done

it as a toughie – lots of steps, hills and rough terrain. And similarly to Grizzly about an hour's drive further west in Seaton, Devon (see also page 154), it's always had a race name. In the 2004 and the eleventh edition of the race, it was called Legs Eleven. Then, in 2015, it was named The Call of the Wild.

The race starts and finishes in Corfe Common, against the backdrop of Corfe Castle, a thousand-year-old royal stronghold situated in the middle of the Isle of Purbeck peninsula. Once we were off, we did a short loop that was designed to spread the field out a bit, as there was a danger of it getting congested at the various stiles you had to hop over. This also gave an opportunity for spectators to catch a second glance of their runners before they disappeared behind a hill.

Hills play a fairly prominent role in this race: hills, steps and stiles. Up and down we went, on a roller coaster of undulation on every type of terrain known to man, from grassy fields

Corfe Castle.

OPPOSITE: One of the main highlights of the race – Emmetts Hill.

RIGHT: Luckily, there are lots of steps to help you climb Emmetts Hill – around 200 – carved into the hillside.

to rocky single track, and everything else in between. It was hard work but the really hard bits were still to come.

Passing through the quaint town of Worth Matravers and the old quarry of Winspit (once featured in the *Doctor Who* TV series), with the hills of West Man and East Man flanking us, we hit the limestone cliffs of the Jurassic Coast.

OPPOSITE: After the quad-busting climb up Emmetts Hill, any flat bits are a welcome reprieve.

BELOW: Chapman's Pool on the Isle of Purbeck.

The Emmetts Hill stretch down towards Chapman's Pool is like a giant staircase etched into the side of the cliff face. Ridiculously steep and treacherous in places, any relief in reaching the bottom several hundred steps later vanished in a flash, as after a quick water stop we began to immediately trudge our way back up the other side. Now I understood why this was called The Beast!

Heading away from the coast, I had hoped the worst of the hills was over. Sadly not, as a gentle but long incline led us towards the village of Kingston, slowly sapping our legs of what energy might have been left in them. Even the water stop and a quick slurp of a gel did nothing to restore my energy levels. But then I caught a glimpse of Corfe Castle in the distance. Like a beacon, it lured me in, empowering me with the knowledge that I could make it. As I made my way to the pub with my family, clutching my new T-shirt, colour gradually returning to my face, the little grey matter in my head started buzzing, 'Right! Now, what's next?'

Top tips

- Well worth making a weekend out of it. There's so much to see on the Jurassic Coast
- Work on strengthening your quads — you'll need them when powering up the steps from Hell!

ADIDAS THUNDER RUN

Catton Hall,
Swadlincote,
Derbyshire, UK   〜〜 Trail   📅 July   🌐 www.tr24.co.uk

DISTANCE

10K LOOPS
(DISTANCE DEPENDS ON HOW MANY YOU CAN RUN)

LAPS

`0 0 0 0 3 5`

MOST NUMBER OF LAPS (MIXED)

`0 0 0 0 2 9`

TOBIAS' TEAM IN LAPS

99%
COMPLETION
RATE

'Tobias, you're up next!' my teammate Kieran whispered.

As I lay in my tent, listening to the intermittent thunder interspersed with flashes of lightning, I had a sudden memory of my Army days at Sandhurst when told I was now 'on stag' – meaning it was my turn to man the sentry. Perhaps I could pretend that I was asleep, or not even in the tent at all. For the past few hours, rather than sleeping in between my turn on the course, I'd been listening to it raining cats and dogs, interspersed with roars of thunder and brilliant lightning, illuminating the ground like a floodlight. But then again, rain, thunder and lightning, it's all par for the course in the 24-hour race known as the Thunder Run.

'What time is it?' I groaned back.

'3 a.m.,' he replied. 'We've got about twenty minutes before Simon gets back. You better hurry up!'

I was supposed to be up earlier. Springing out of my sleeping bag, I hastily threw on my wet clothes and stepped out of the tent, only to see hundreds of people milling about, chatting.

The adidas Thunder Run, or 'TR24' as it's also known, is a 24-hour off-road relay race where your enemy is the clock. It takes place in the grounds of the stately home of Catton Hall, on the borders of Staffordshire and South Derbyshire, which over the weekend is transformed into a mini Glastonbury, at the centre of which is a 10K undulating off-road loop that twists and turns around the 250-acre estate.

The format of the race is straightforward: run as many 10km laps as possible within 24 hours. Before you turn the page, thinking there's no way you can run for that long, there are plenty of ways you can enter, the most popular option being as a team of five or eight. This can be a male, female or a mixed team, where at least one member must be of the opposite sex. Moreover, every team member must complete at least one lap. Some suckers for punishment choose the solo or pairs options, with the winners clocking as many as 20 laps. Regardless, the team or individual within their category who completes the most number of laps at the moment the clock stops will win.

Most teams send their best runners off first in order to get a decent head start.

Since the race began in 2009, it's been heavily oversubscribed, and received as many as 10,000 entries for one of 2,500 places in 2015. It attracts a wide range of enthusiasts, from running and triathlon clubs, work colleagues looking to do some team building, friends from school, or those individuals who simply want to find out how far they can run in 24 hours. What's more, you can even bring your family and friends to support as there is free camping.

Within moments of joining my Mixed Team of Eight (whom I had not met before) at the makeshift campsite sitting on the edge of the 10-km course, we were already forging friendships and coming up with ideas as to how best to tackle this 24-hour challenge. The rules state one person must be on the course at all times, but that individual can do more than one lap if they choose. Rather than going for the conventional method of taking turns to run, we'd work in pairs, each doing two laps in four and therefore allowing more or less 10 hours to rest – a plan that worked jolly well, except when it came to getting up in the middle of the night during a thunderstorm.

The course is a combination of woods, steep hills and very twisty single track, making it sometimes difficult to overtake or build up any speed. During the day, it was hot and the ground was hard and unforgiving. We'd each do a full lap, before handing over the 'baton' – a bracelet – to our teammate.

In between laps, we'd hang out in the well-equipped food tents, grab a complementary massage or clean up in the hot showers. And

in the beautiful warm summer weather it was heavenly. However, as day turned to night, we donned our head torches just as the torrential rain began to fall, turning the hard-packed ground into a squelching quagmire. Things then got more serious … and more fun. With people slipping and sliding all over the place and more than one person jumping out of their skin as enormous bolts of lightning (helpfully) lit up the ground around us, at times it felt more like a mud run than a 24-hour race.

By midday on Sunday, 24 hours after we'd started, we'd each run at least a marathon or more, totalling 29 laps, putting us seventh overall in the Mixed Teams of Eight category (out of 253 teams). To put it mildly, we were chuffed to bits – it's not every race where you start out as strangers but finish not only as friends, but a team. It was a great experience.

The start is more akin to a 10K cross-country race rather than one that goes on for 24 hours.

Top tips

- Bring a powerful head torch (and carry a back-up)
- Don't forget to stay fuelled and hydrated. You'll be running for a long time
- Pack spare running clothes and shoes. No one likes putting on wet kit!

THE UK WIFE CARRYING RACE

The Nower, Dorking, UK ﹀﹀ Field 15+m 📅 March 🌐 www.trionium.com/wife

DISTANCE

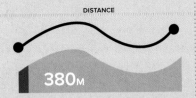

380M

0 0 0 0 0 6 TH
TOBIAS' FINISHING POSITION

99%
COMPLETION
RATE

When I asked my then-girlfriend, Zayne, if she'd be my 'wife' in the UK Wife Carrying Championships, there was a certain amount of apprehension on her part. Not least because we weren't married (in fact you don't need to use your own wife; you can 'borrow' one), but even more so when I demonstrated to her the 'Estonian Hold' – the preferred method when in a rush for carrying your mistress.

This involves sticking your head in between your wife's legs and lifting her up, so her head is now facing your bottom. However, upon various exclamations about how she was getting a rush of blood to her head in between fits of giggles, we decided that it was only 380m after all. How hard could it be? Well, according to the website, it might be fatal:

Wife carrying can be a dangerous activity, which can lead to any one or more of the following injuries: slipped disk, broken legs and arms, spinal damage, facial injury, skull fractures, hernias, and other sundry injuries and illnesses, and potentially including death. But please don't let this put you off!

Fast forward a few months and Zayne is standing on a set of scales, feeling like a jockey at a weigh-in, whilst looking at me with one of those withering expressions that tells me I'm in trouble.

'It's pretty close,' they said, staring at the needle that was hovering around the 50kg mark. 'But on this occasion, I think you're OK!' On any other day, telling your wife that she's potentially 'underweight' might be a good thing, but today, she had to weigh a minimum of 50kg, or else we'd need to find a few cans of baked beans to bring us up to score. But at the other end of the spectrum, the person carrying the heaviest wife is awarded a pound of sausages – for 'strength' – which means there's a good chance they'll also win the ceremonial tin of dog food and a pot

The 'wives' wear helmets as protection, less they are dropped on their heads by their careless husbands.

noodle for being the slowest competitors.

A few moments later, we're standing on the start line alongside 30 other couples – all looking slightly bemused, especially our wives. To add to the indignation of being weighed like a prize cow, our 'wives' had to wear cycle helmets – something the style-conscious amongst them might object to. However, we all decided looking like a dork is better than what would happen if we were to drop our respective 'wives' on their heads. And then factor in the BBC film crew and photographers waiting to catch our every move and we felt pretty much on show.

'Have you practised much?' asked the couple next to us, as they watched me insert my head between Zayne's legs and hoist her over my shoulders. We told them that our only practice run had been down our corridor at home, where I almost gave Zayne an aneurysm.

Perhaps we should have practised a little more, because I discovered that wife carrying takes a certain amount of skill. From the moment we were given the off, I felt like a little kid competing in the school's annual Father and Son race.

Zayne had decided, perhaps out of fear, to hold onto my shorts rather than my waist, which had the effect of making it even more awkward to run. And her squeezing my head like a walnut in a vice-like grip was not helping matters, either!

Whilst everyone else jumped over the hay bales (cunningly placed a bit like a steeple chase), I clambered over them ungracefully whilst Zayne giggled uncontrollably as she informed me that everyone was overtaking us. By the time we'd reached the turnaround point, I was ready to drop Zayne and make her walk. Naively, I'd dismissed the 15m of ascent which I'd read about on the website – it's not exactly a mountain – but with a 'wife' wrapped around my neck, it felt like I was climbing one.

Thankfully, the descent was quicker, despite the crowds gleefully tossing buckets of water over us as we made our way over the hay bales, crossing the line in sixth position. If I'd had my senses about me I should have asked her to marry me there and then. It would have made for an even better story. Sadly, any sense I might have had departed me on the first hay bale. Now married, we look back on our first race together and wonder if we could do better.

There's always the Wife Carrying World Championships in Finland!

Top tips

- Don't drop your wife – she won't appreciate it
- Find a wife as light as possible
- The Estonian Hold is the quickest and most popular method for carrying your wife

Although ungainly, the Estonian Hold is the preferred method for carrying your wife.

9

KNACKER CRACKER 10K

 **Box Hill,
Surrey, UK**

 Cross-country

 1 January

🌐 **www.trionium.com/knackercracker**

DISTANCE

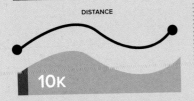

10K

	HR	MIN	SEC
	0 0	4 5	5 1

FASTEST TIME (KNOWN)

0 0	4 7	3 5

TOBIAS' FINISHING TIME

99% COMPLETION RATE

It's fair to say that for the majority of people New Year's Day generally starts off quite slowly – a groggy head, a cup of coffee, a morning walk, pub lunch, quiet siesta, a spot of TV, bed … But for some, New Year's Day is also a time to kick-start those resolutions, which often revolve around getting fitter and healthier. What better way to start the year than kicking off with a race? And if ever there was a race to put a grin (or grimace) on your face, it's the Knacker Cracker 10K.

OK, perhaps the saner amongst you might not choose a race referred to as 'Britain's toughest 10K', but hey, you might as well start on a high! And if you live in the southeast of England, a great place to get high is the National Trust-owned Box Hill.

The first time I heard about the Knacker Cracker was from a chap I'd met at the finish of The Grim Challenge (see also page 34). He told me about this crazy event on New Year's Day

It could just be a hat or a full-on squirrel outfit, but fancy dress is very much the done thing at this event.

that involved running up and down Box Hill in fancy dress. If I liked The Grim Challenge, then I'd love the Knacker Cracker, he figured. Considering I've now done the race three times, he must have been right.

As soon as I'd cast an eye over the incredibly basic 'says what it is on the tin' website, I was already hooked. With the promise of a personalised race T-shirt (with our names on the back), a medal and a mug, and all for less than £30, it was also a bargain. As with any race, it's very easy to sign up for something and promptly forget that it follows the biggest night of the year, though. And even with a relaxed 11 a.m. start, just getting out of bed, clearing your groggy head and making your way to the start line requires a certain stamina. But having foolishly decided to host

a New Year's Eve Party and therefore last man to bed, I arrived at the start line in a fatigued and somewhat delicate state and was quickly overtaken by a man dressed as Pac-Man, a bottle of champagne and a Spartan warrior, amongst others, many teasingly tut-tutting me for my tardiness and, more to the point, for not wearing fancy dress!

Indeed, of the three times I've now taken part in this event, it's much more fun when you've made the effort to dress up. Moreover, of these three occasions, the course has changed every time, with the guarantee that at some point you will be reduced to a walk, even if it's for just a few moments. Because, regardless of the exact route, you'll be doing a heck of a lot

of climbing – around 500m worth – a significant figure for a 10K.

If there is one part of the course that will rattle your brains, it will probably be the Eiger Steps, which you not only have to go down but also go back up. As one person observed: 'The steps at the end were actually loaned to the National Trust by Satan himself.'

But the fresh air and endorphins of chasing a champagne bottle gave me renewed energy and by some fluke, I managed to finish up on the podium. As I stood to accept my prize of a bottle of white wine for third place (probably the last thing in the world I wanted at that precise moment!), I couldn't help but feel lucky to have stumbled upon such a cracking race.

Top tips

- Aim to get to the start at least 30 minutes early
- Wear fancy dress – at the minimum a funny hat (there's a prize for the fastest in fancy dress and for the best costume)
- Wear trail shoes (but no spikes) – it's muddy in places and you'll slip on the grass.

OPPOSITE: The piper playing in the runners on their final descent down Box Hill to the finish.

BELOW: Some years, runners start at the bottom, run to the top of the hill and then run back down again before continuing up the Zig Zag road. Cruel.

10 PARKRUN

 Worldwide ᎷᎷᎷ Variable 📅 Every Saturday at 9 a.m. 🌐 www.parkrun.org.uk

DISTANCE

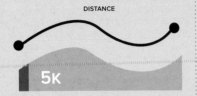

5K

	HR		MIN		SEC	
0	0	1	3	4	8	

FASTEST TIME (BUSHEY PARK AND WORLDWIDE)

| 0 | 0 | 1 | 6 | 5 | 4 |

TOBIAS' FINISHING TIME (PB)

99% COMPLETION RATE

Over 65,000 events, more than 127,000 volunteers worldwide, 651 parks spread across 11 countries and over 1 million runners … it is fair to say that unless you've been living in a cave for the past ten years, you must have heard of Parkrun. And if you haven't, then you've been missing out on one of the best running events ever created. What's more, Parkrun is 100 per cent free to enter.

Held every Saturday at 9 a.m., more than 60,000 runners around the world gather at one of the 651 (and counting) locations to run a 5km time trial. Each event is run by a group of local volunteers who will help with marshalling, scanning the barcodes (which record your time) or operating the timer. Almost all of them are runners themselves.

As an incentive to encourage you to do more and more Parkruns and, hopefully better your PB, they've created a clever system of milestone targets: 10 (Juniors only), 50, 100, 250 and even 500. When you reach a milestone indicating you've run that number of Parkruns, you will be awarded a coloured T-shirt that displays your membership to this exclusive club, which you will proudly wear whenever you do a Parkrun.

You might think that membership of the different clubs sounds difficult to achieve, but to put it in perspective, at the time of writing, worldwide more than 27,000 Juniors had reached the 10 Club, 25,000 people were members of the 50 Club, a further 8,300 had run more than 100 Parkruns, an incredible 262 had run more than 250, and one superhuman person (Darren Wood) has completed more

than 500 Parkruns. Considering over half of Darren's runs were at Bushy Park in Teddington, Middlesex, it makes sense that if you were to choose just one Parkrun to do before you die, then it should be Bushy Park – the very first Parkrun to be set up.

It all began on Saturday, 2 October 2004 when, led by Paul Sinton-Hewitt and the other Parkrun founders, 13 runners gathered for the inaugural event. Initially called the Bushy Park Time Trial, there was no expectation that it would grow beyond the boundaries of the park. But within two years, those initial 13 runners had multiplied to 378, at which point it was decided to trial a simultaneous Parkrun at another location. So, with a certain degree

Runners listen to the pre-race briefing on Lime Avenue in Bushy Park, with the Diana Memorial in the background.

More than 1,000 people can be expected at Bushy Park.

of trepidation, the Wimbledon Common Time Trial (later Wimbledon Common Parkrun) was launched on 6 January 2007 and by the end of the year, seven events were being held around the UK and even one in Zimbabwe.

You'll first need to register on the Parkrun website and print out the unique barcode which they'll scan at the end to record your time. The Bushy Park start is on the eastern side of the Diana Fountain – which you won't fail to miss, thanks to the several hundred chatty runners who'll be joining you. There's a high turnout of club runners, local and from afar. In fact, nowadays, over 29,000 runners from almost 1,000 clubs have taken part in the Bushy Parkrun.

As anyone who has previously visited Bushy Park will tell you, it's fairly flat and therefore a good location for PBs (the course and world record stands at 13:48, set by Team GB Olympian Andrew Baddeley). The route resembles a figure of eight and stays in the northeastern quadrant of the park, following a mixture of surfaces, including grass, trail and tarmac. Being the Royal Ascot of Parkruns, you'll find a range of runners, from elite athletes to your recreational runner and a smattering of mums running with push buggies. Regardless, as soon as the obligatory briefing is over, fingers will be on watches, as everyone gets ready to start.

Those at the front hurtle off as though doing a 100m sprint, leaving others in less of a hurry to make their way around at a slightly gentler pace. To me it felt akin to a cross-country race, as participants bound across the grass, following Nightingale Lane towards the cricket club at Hampton Wick, which you circumnavigate

If it's a hot day, the shade from the woods can be a welcome respite.

before heading towards the aptly named Leg of Mutton Pond. A sharp right turn and you hit a track, making your way towards Sandy Lane Gate, then following the perimeter of the park before heading back towards the centre, another turn and ultimately the finish.

As you go through the finish chute, you'll be handed a token, which you take with you to the timekeepers, who will scan your barcode (most people carry these strung around their necks on a laminated card). Within an hour, as you enjoy a coffee and celebrate your achievements in the post-run social at The Pheasantry Cafe, you'll receive a text telling you your time, position and whether you've PB'd.

At that exact moment, you'll be reborn as a Parkrunner and start to wonder if you could get to the first 50 Club milestone. Believe me, Parkrun is not only addictive, but for many it's a way of life. It is a gift from runners to runners.

Top tips

- Many people laminate their barcode, which you can hang around your neck. Otherwise it's easy to lose
- Study the course description closely so you're familiar with where you're going – especially if you're fast!

11 THE GHERKIN CHALLENGE

📍 30 St Mary Axe, London EC3 ⌇ Concrete steps 🏢 180m 📅 September 🌐 www.nspcc.org.uk/what-you-can-do/events/the-gherkin-challenge

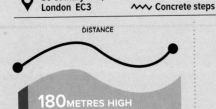

DISTANCE

180METRES HIGH

HR   MIN   SEC
0 0 0 5 1 4
FASTEST TIME (KNOWN)

0 0 0 5 2 6
TOBIAS' FINISHING TIME

99% COMPLETION RATE

Although the shortest race in this book, somewhat surprisingly The Gherkin Challenge is one of the most brutal. Your legs will course with lactic acid, your head will spin to the point where you're dizzy, your lungs will burn as if on fire and you'll sweat more than a fox with a limp. Even after you've finished, you won't stop coughing for half an hour. Welcome to the world of tower running!

Some might argue that in the UK we're vertically challenged, with neither our mountains nor our skyscrapers gaining many accolades in the height department. At a meagre 180m the Gherkin is nothing compared to New York's 381m Empire State Building or Taiwan's 509m high 101 Tower, believe me. But when you look up at 30 St Mary Axe, otherwise known as 'The Gherkin', it's hard to imagine wanting to climb anything higher than its 38 floors.

Outside of the UK, tower running has become so popular that there's even a Towerrunning World Cup and a rival Vertical World Circuit, where over 100,000 of the fittest men and women on the planet practically leap up staircases as if they were running on the flat. It's fiercely competitive.

Unlike it's big brother across the pond, the Empire State Building Run-Up, which has a mass start, The Gherkin Challenge has staggered waves throughout the day, with competitors setting off in pairs at 5-second intervals. The fastest are encouraged to go first to avoid having to overtake people on the stairs.

Having bade farewell to my wife, who was sensibly taking the elevator to the top, where she would hopefully meet me later on, I stood at the front of the wave, wondering how on earth I should pace myself. It's obviously tempting to take two steps at a time, but this puts huge strain on your quads and eventually, you'll start to slow down. The other option is to take it one step at a time, which

The 180m high Gherkin –
one of London's most iconic
buildings.

Top tips

- Train by taking the
  stairs wherever
  you go

- Using the hand
  rails to propel
  yourself around
  the stairs can
  help, but caution
  needs to be
  exercised

- Two steps is
  quicker but
  more tiring

can be quite slow but at least you won't burn out.

As soon as I was given the signal to go, I leapt forward like a hound, bounding up the stairs two at a time – despite my best intentions not to do so. Before the race, someone had advised using the banisters to swing myself around, to keep the momentum, which after ten floors was beginning to ebb. Of course, being in an emergency stairwell, there's not a lot to look at as you run, nor are your friends and family there to cheer you on and offer moral support. You're instead relying on NSPCC volunteers, scattered on various floors, for some measure of encouragement – or at least to stop you making an early exit!

Within a few minutes, I'd started to slow down and began to perspire quite heavily. My quads were burning and I was beginning to feel a little faint, probably not helped by the fact that there's not much ventilation. As expected, taking two steps at a time was wearing me out, so I reduced down to one step, which suddenly felt very odd. But sure enough, I began to catch up with the younger guy who'd started with me and had disconcertingly disappeared several moments earlier, his footsteps and heavy breathing the only sign I wasn't alone. By the time I passed him, youthful enthusiasm had taken its toll and he was looking pretty knackered – as was I!

Feeling as if hours had passed, but in reality only 5 minutes and 26 seconds later, I climbed the last of the 1,037 steps and popped out on the 38th floor, practically falling into the arms of my wife. In between catching my breath and a minor coughing fit, I gazed in wonder at London sprawled out beneath my feet. If ever there was motivation to climb one of the city's highest buildings, the view from the top and an accompanying glass of champagne is worth it.

Thirty-eight floors, and almost 180 vertical metres later, you approach the finish line.

12 THE LONDON MARATHON_

London, UK 〰 Road 📅 April 🌐 www.virginmoneylondonmarathon.com

DISTANCE

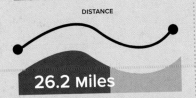

26.2 Miles

HR		MIN		SEC	
0	2	0	4	2	9

FASTEST TIME (KNOWN)

0	2	4	9	5	8

TOBIAS' FINISHING TIME

98.7% COMPLETION RATE

'Marathon running used to be done by slightly mad people,' race director Hugh Brasher once said, 'but now running is the second most popular recreation in Britain.'

And if ever there was one race that's helped raise this statistic, set dozens of world records and not done too badly out of the running boom, it would be The London Marathon – the race that Hugh's father, Olympic champion Chris Brasher, founded. It is my local marathon and a race that I have grown to love over the six years I've run it. And alongside being one of the World Majors it is without doubt one of the greatest marathons of them all – and where Paula Radcliffe set the female world record of 2:15:25 in 2003.

Since the race first launched in 1981, more than 900,000 people have completed it, which is an extraordinary statistic when you consider how difficult it is to get an entry. The ballot system has changed many times over the years and nowadays, you need to enter during the two-week window immediately after the previous race, finding out in October whether you have been lucky.

The other option, and the one I used to gain my place in my first 2005 London (which was also my first ever marathon), was to apply through one of the hundreds of charities who use the marathon as a crucial part of their fundraising campaigns. As the largest annual fundraising event in the world, it's a course of action that many take and the race to date has raised a Guinness World Record, making £716 million and counting. However, a word of caution: raising the minimum sum of money (I had to raise £1,500) can be more stressful than training for the race itself.

The final option, for those who have bad luck in ballots and yet have a modicum of running talent, is to try and qualify for a 'Good for Age' category, achieved by running a sub 3.05 marathon (if you're a man less than 40 years of age) or 3.45 if you're a woman. And if none of these options work, then you could apply through a British Athletics Associated

Running over Tower Bridge is definitely one of the best highlights of the race.

running club, who are allocated a number of guaranteed places.

Having trained like a lunatic, and travelled to the deepest, darkest and furthest reaches of London to collect your bib number, you then have to make your way to the start. Luckily, by way of some consolation, all runners are entitled to free travel to the start on Southeastern trains from Charing Cross, Waterloo East, Cannon Street, London Bridge and Victoria.

Although the majority of the club and charity runners will proudly display their respective singlets, this is a race that embraces fancy dress. Hundreds set out to break Guinness World Records for their chosen theme, whether a superhero or a rhino (one man even carried a fridge on his back!). Sadly, there is now a time limit of eight hours to complete the race, which means that those wishing to sport a more cumbersome outfit, such as an antique deep-sea diving suit, might have to look elsewhere (Lloyd Scott took five days, eight hours in 2002).

I don't think I've ever run a race where every single mile of the course is lined with supporters – often over a million people. You'll pass cheering late-night revellers still clinging to their pints of beer, charity stands with irrepressible levels of enthusiasm for their runners, running clubs, along with friends and family. Many will get up early to find the best viewing spots to catch sight of the elite runners at the business end of the race as well as the celebrities, club runners, charity entrants and rhinos bringing up the rear.

It's also a fantastic race for sightseeing, as you run by a raft of well known landmarks:

> ## Top tips
> - Allow plenty of time to get to the start (public transport can get congested)
> - Write your name on your running shirt – this allows supporters to cheer you on by name

the Royal Artillery Barracks, the London Eye, the Houses of Parliament, the City of London, Canary Wharf, Tower Bridge and of course Buckingham Palace, to name just a few. And with the event being broadcast in 196 countries, you'll see dozens of camera crews with helicopters flying overhead. It's pretty impressive stuff.

The levels of support and buzzing atmosphere make this race one that should lend itself perfectly to a PB. Although not particularly flat (there are a couple of inclines that might slow you a little), the numerous aid stations supplying water and sports drinks and the constant support of people cheering your name (if you've written it on your T-shirt) will keep you going well beyond the finish line.

Which just so happens to be on the most famous road in London – The Mall. With Buckingham Palace as a backdrop, you'll feel like a million dollars as you run down the final stretch, even if your quads won't be thanking you. After collecting the coveted medal you've worked so hard for, along with your goody bag (with one-size-fits-all-T-shirt), when your family and friends ask you how it was, hopefully you'll be grinning from ear to ear, wondering why on earth you haven't done this race sooner.

With only a couple of miles left, the spectators crowd around Parliament Square to offer support.

13 GREEN BELT RELAY

Greater London, UK Footpath, trail, road 1,769m (estimate) May 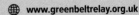 www.greenbeltrelay.org.uk

DISTANCE

220 Miles

HR	MIN	SEC
2 1	2 8	0 0

FASTEST TIME (COURSE RECORD)

99% COMPLETION RATE

One of the many positive aspects of running is that it gives you a very valid excuse to join a club of equally enthusiastic and like-minded individuals. And one of the best races in which to put this whole concept into practice is the Green Belt Relay, a 22-stage relay race designed with running clubs in mind. The seed of the idea was born in 1995, when London running club the Stragglers, mapped out a course that takes in 220 miles of the Green Belt around the outside of London, all in a single weekend.

Lest you think this sounds daunting, don't worry! Each club puts forward a team of 11 individuals, usually with anything from 35 to 50 teams taking part. A runner will take on one of the 11 stages on Saturday and Sunday, with the longest being just over 13 miles and the shortest just under six. Unsurprisingly, there's a keen competitive element amongst the clubs, although team spirit and great camaraderie are the real underpinning of this event.

The runners themselves are of varying standards and by and large, the stages are allocated according to each individual's strengths. In order to give a fair balance, each stage has a difficulty rating out of 10. My friends know that I'm a sucker for punishment and so on the Saturday I found myself allocated the 12.2-mile run from Little Marlow, with a rating of 10. Typical!

This stage turned out to be far from easy, swinging up and around High Wycombe and through the glorious Chilterns. But once I'd settled into the rhythm I began to thoroughly enjoy myself. I should say that 80 per cent of the route is off-road, following footpaths, bridle paths or quiet country lanes. And although well marked, that doesn't mean there's no opportunity of getting lost! Which is why you're encouraged to download the route to your GPS and carry a map – just in case.

Minibuses collect each runner at their start and finish stage, where you join up with your fellow club members and compare stories, plus fill up on well-earned refreshments. By Saturday evening, the clubs temporarily go their separate ways, ready to settle into a comfortable hotel and a hearty meal, to prepare for Day 2 on Sunday morning. With an event of this type, it's inevitable that you spend quite a bit of time on

The relay starts at Hampton Court Palace.

a minibus. Some team members are grateful to go first, thus allowing you to relax for the rest of the day, but of course if you're one of the last to run, then it can be a long wait.

Box Hill, as I know only too well, is decidedly hilly but it still remains one of my favourite runs and each time I go there I appreciate something new. I was therefore delighted when I was given this section on the Sunday. My part of the route followed much of the North Downs Way, and being ranked 9/10 in terms of difficulty, gave me a good run for my money. By the end of the afternoon, when the last runner had set off for the final stage from Walton Bridge, it was simply a case of making best speed back to the Hawker Centre, not far from Hampton Court Palace.

As ever, the atmosphere at the finish was one of jubilation. The speed of each runner in the relay was calculated and the sum total added up before the overall team winner could be decided. On this occasion it was not my club – the Clapham Chasers – we came fourth. But regardless of what position we came, every single one of us had a great time. After all, how often do you get to run around the Green Belt of London in a single weekend?

Top tips

- Research your section of the leg in advance. It's easy to take a wrong turn when in a rush
- Although it's perfectly possible to create your own team, it's far easier to join a club who have experience of organising the logistics

14 WINGS FOR LIFE
WORLD RUN

📍 **Silverstone, UK and worldwide**　　〜〜 **Road**　　📅 **May**　　🌐 **www.wingsforlifeworldrun.com**

15K AVERAGE DISTANCE

```
0 0 7 9 . 9 0 K
```
WINNING DISTANCE (WORLDWIDE)

```
0 0 6 9 . 3 7 K
```
WINNING DISTANCE (UK)

```
0 0 3 8 . 0 0 K
```
TOBIAS' DISTANCE

99% COMPLETION RATE

As anyone who's done an ultra-marathon will tell you, running is as much a mental game as a physical one: your mind will be telling you to give up long before your body starts to protest. So if you really want to test your grit, both mentally and physically, then the Wings for Life World Run might be just what you're looking for.

The last time I'd visited Silverstone race-track, I watched dozens of Formula One cars scream their way around the track, battling it out for supremacy on the grid. Now, I myself was standing on the start grid amongst 645 runners, nervously chatting to each other before the official start time of 11 a.m. Also parked on the line was a shiny white Land Rover Discovery – a vehicle each and every one of us would see again before the end of the race.

Spanning six continents, 32 countries and 13 time zones, as the name suggests the Wings for life World Run is not just limited to those of us gathered at Silverstone. As we lined up,

as many as 45,000 runners, aged anywhere between 18 and 91, were simultaneously taking part in this global event. And not only is the race global, but it also has a particular unique twist.

'How far do you hope to run?' I ask my friend Simon, whilst we limber up.

'I've absolutely no idea,' he tells me. 'But all I know is if we want to run a marathon, we need to make it in less than 3:08.'

Simon has a marathon PB of 2:37 and I too have run a fair few sub-three hours, so this wasn't an unreasonable target. But neither of us had factored in just how hilly the course would be, nor the mental effects of the previously alluded to 'twist'.

There's no static finish line! Rather, we're being chased by a 'Catcher Car' that will eliminate runners one by one until there is only one of us left in the UK, and ultimately one left in the entire world.

As the sport director Nick Gracie explained to me before the race, 'Having a "Catcher Car" is a nice concept and mentally it makes it a bit more challenging. You just have to go as hard as you can, as opposed to as hard as you *think* you can.'

At precisely 11 a.m., like a herd of speeding gazelles, we did just that, dashing off around Silverstone race track as though our lives depended on it. However, our enthusiasm might have been a bit premature – the 'Catcher Car' wasn't to leave for another 30 minutes.

Top tips

- Calculate how far you think you can go and make that your goal
- Mentally prepare yourself – it's harder than a normal race
- Remember, you're raising funds for over 3 million people with spinal cord injuries

No matter how fast you are, the Chaser Car will always catch you, some earlier than others.

Eight and a half kilometres into the race and we left the confines of the track, heading north towards the village of Silverstone and beyond. The 100km route – that's the maximum distance – would follow an anti-clockwise loop along traffic-free closed roads through the Northamptonshire countryside. Initially, we sped along, encouraged by local residents who turned out to cheer and encourage us. The atmosphere was buoyant. But a combination of nasty hills and warm weather meant that after a couple of hours we'd begun to slow down. Then Simon announced he'd had enough and urged me to keep going.

Now, I was playing a mental battle: it would be so easy to stop and wait for the car to catch me. 'Surely it would get to me soon,' I thought.

I was quite ready to take a seat on the 'pick-up bus' collecting stragglers caught by the car. Then I reminded myself I was running against the world and for a good cause – the spinal cord research foundation, Wings for Life, after which the race was named. Knowing that 100 per cent of the profits were going to the charity, thanks to Red Bull's sponsorship, was a motivating factor.

Eventually, like death and taxes, the car closed in behind me. I could hear it hooting long before I saw it. Though I tried to pick up the pace and outrun it, I was fighting a losing battle. What really smarted, though, was to

OPPOSITE: Silverstone Circuit in Northamptonshire.

BELOW: A runner being passed by the Catcher Car.

be caught at 38km – half the distance of the global winner. I'd not even managed to run a marathon. But when I jumped onto the bus, to my surprise I was greeted with a round of applause from the other runners. It turned out I was the thirteenth left on the course! Later, I'd discover that I was 375th in the world.

With this race the whole point is not knowing where the finish lies: you might run much further than you think or, as in my case, far less. Regardless, either way one of two things will happen – either you run out of gas or the car catches you, although if fate has its way, the car will be the one to run out of gas.

ZOMBIE EVACUATION RACE

Various locations, UK

 Various

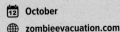 **Trail**

October

zombieevacuation.com

DISTANCE

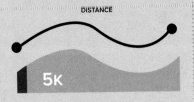

5K

0 0 0 0 0 2 ND

TOBIAS' FINISHING POSITION (SURVIVOR)

99% COMPLETION RATE

It wasn't the first time I'd stared into the face of a zombie, and nor would it be the last as things were going. With blood smeared all over his face, he snarls at me before letting out an agonising scream. This is possibly due to the fact that he's missing his left arm, or perhaps he's realised he's stuck in the woods and unable to find his way out. I run towards him, feinting a move to the right before going left to avoid his deadly clutches.

Zombie racing has become so popular that it's now almost become a sport in its own right. What makes this race unusual (besides the obvious zombie factor) is that for many people, this was their first race of any kind. They were put off by the competitive nature of your average 5K or 10K, but the idea of being chased by zombies sounded fun. Moreover, and this is really one of its major selling points, the race relies on a hoard of zombie volunteers. So, if you want to involve the family in your weekend antics, you can sign up for the race and they can dress up as the undead and chase you. In this they will be assisted by professional make-up artists with the ability to transform the most unassuming and charming individual into a very dead-looking monster. And with a couple of lessons on how to moan and groan with conviction as well as hiss and growl, they become very convincing.

However, if you're reading this book, you're probably more keen to race than chase so let's move on to the event itself. On arrival you are greeted by a Sergeant Ormroyd of his Majesty's RAZORs (Royal Armoured Zombie Outbreak Response Unit), who regretfully informs you (as if it's any surprise) that the nation is in a state of lockdown after a zombie epidemic outbreak. Your only hope of salvation is to reach the 'evacuation zone' – which just so

Zombie medics chasing Tobias.

Professional make-up artists help to create very realistic looking zombies.

happens to be 5km away. The major snag is that the route is riddled with obstacles and hoards of the undead, all of whom are intent on 'biting' you and turning you into one of their own, something they can achieve by removing all three of your life tags (small luminescent Velcro tags attached to a belt round your waist). It quickly becomes apparent 'only the fittest will survive' this ordeal and win the survivor's medal. Those unsuccessful will be awarded the 'infected medal' and escorted to the 'Neutralisation zone to be terminated'.

Although you're initially led off by Sergeant Ormroyd and his soldiers, and thus have a sense of false security, just a few minutes later you come under attack. From that moment on, you're on your own as you run for dear life.

When I did the inaugural Zombie Evacuation Race, held then at Pippingford Park in East Sussex and now at Allianz Park Stadium, Greenlands Lane, London NW4, I was naturally new to Zombie racing and

Some zombies are more troublesome than others.

the strategies of not being infected. Being somewhat fitter than most of the other competitors, I quickly found myself on my own facing 20 zombies, all eager for the first bite of flesh. Knackered from jumping over obstacles and trudging muddy fields, playing British Bulldog with the undead proved to be too much and eventually I lost all of my lifelines. Besides meaning that I was now infected, it also made it less fun as I was essentially no longer 'fleeing for my life' but simply running a tough 5K. But if you do happen to lose a life or all three of them, you can find hidden medical packs with a vaccine that will restore one of your life tags – easier said than done when armed zombies are trying to bite you.

Top tips

- Don't go out too fast, otherwise you'll find yourself on your own
- Embrace the event for what it is and aim to have fun rather than race
- Prepare to get covered in fake blood!

Whether you love dressing up or simply enjoy the thrill of being scared, the Zombie Evacuation Race is about the most fun you can have over 5K. It doesn't pretend to take itself seriously, and nor should you. If you embrace the spirit of the event, you'll be laughing and howling your way to the finish – hopefully as a 'survivor'.

16 PARIS MARATHON

Paris, France   Road   12 April   www.schneiderelectricparismarathon.com

DISTANCE

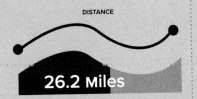

26.2 Miles

	HR	MIN	SEC
FASTEST TIME (KNOWN)	02	05	04
TOBIAS' FINISHING TIME	02	55	00

98% COMPLETION RATE

'Allez, *allez*, Tobias!' the Frenchman shouted at me from the pavement besides the Avenue des Champs-Elysées. I was a bit startled by his somewhat energetic cries of support considering I was only a few minutes into the Marathon de Paris and with 26 odd miles still to go, but this is France, a country where cheering is practically a national pastime whether it be towards runners or, as is more often the case, cyclists during the Tour de France.

You could say that the Paris Marathon, as English-speaking folk would refer to it, is the rival to the London Marathon – two countries connected by a tunnel, two capitals linked by a train, each with 40-something thousand runners slogging it through the streets. But there the similarities end.

Getting a slot in the Paris Marathon used to be easier than its London rival and an excellent alternative if you didn't get in on the ballot, but in the past few years runners have cottoned on to this excellent sell-out marathon. Today, to secure a place you need to apply in one of three phases. The biggest slot is in the four-week period after the race. However, it's a case of fingers on buzzers because in 2015 over 22,000 runners secured their 2016 slot in a mere 90 minutes. The second window of opportunity is in September, when the price naturally goes up by €20 or so but competition for places will be every bit as hot.

As is customary in France, if you are French you need a race licence (obtainable from your running club); also a medical certificate that is valid for a year and available from your doctor. Overseas competitors need a valid medical certificate, which you will already have obtained from your local GP, showing you're fit to run. The cost of this totally depends on your doctor. I have paid between £15 and £60. These items are essential when you collect your running bib from the Salon du Running expo at the Porte de Versailles. The medical certificate from your GP can be expensive but you'll get to use it again, as the expo is brilliant at encouraging you to enter more races in France.

Organised by the Amaury Sports Organisation (ASO), the same folk behind the Tour de France, it's a slick affair with all the

pomp and ceremony you'd expect. But with the race starting on the Champs-Elysées, you need to allow time to get there. You can imagine what it must be like trying to be one of 40,000 runners spewing from the nearby Metro, like rats out of a sewer. But as you emerge into daylight and join the throng of runners walking through the Arc de Triomphe, it's impossible not to feel that impalpable thrill of being in Paris.

It doesn't get much better than starting on the Champs-Elysées with the iconic Arc de Triomphe in the background.

If you've not already had a comfort break, now is the moment. Because you have to join the wave based on your aspirational finish time (which, if you're hoping for a sub-three, must be backed up with evidence), faster runners will find themselves far, far away from the portaloos. This is when it's handy to speak

Top tips

- Allow plenty of time to get your medical certificate from your local GP
- Arrange accommodation well in advance, as with so many overseas entries, many hotels are soon booked up

French, as I experienced first-hand when I found myself begging for mercy from a nearby café owner, who kindly took pity and let me in.

As you'd expect of a marathon this size, there are pacesetters – four for every 15 minutes for those looking to finish between 3 hours and 4:40. Having been a pacesetter myself at other races, it's amazing how many people rely on you to get them to the end. The other source of morale is the infamous blue line, marking the exact 42.195 kilometres. Deviate off the blue line and you're essentially running further than you need to. Sadly, although it's meant to last at least a few days, if the weather doesn't hold then you might find it eroding in places.

The centre of Paris is a veritable hotspot of touristic delights and at its most beautiful in spring. In the first half of the race you'll pass the well-known sites of the Musée du Louvre and the Place de la Bastille before entering the Bois de Vincennes, the largest park in Paris and where you'll see the Château de Vincennes, ancient home of the kings of France. As you'd expect in a country that loves its food, the aid stations are packed full of nutritional delicacies, from apples and oranges to nuts and sugar cubes. However, with the sheer quantity of runners passing through, it can

also be a bit of a bun fight as you try not to step on a carpet of discarded banana skins, orange peel and empty cups.

In the second half, you'll end up passing the Bastille again, before following La Seine, passing the Cathédrale Notre-Dame de Paris and the Musée d'Orsay. Here, you'll briefly descend into a tunnel beneath the Place de la Concorde, where a 'rave party' appears to be taking place, before popping out on the other side towards Grand Palais. And of course no marathon in Paris is complete without seeing the breathtaking Eiffel Tower at the 18-mile point, just when you might be beginning to flag a little. And that simply leaves the Bois de Boulogne in the 16th arrondissement before arrival at the finish line.

By rights, you could argue that a capital city race as successful as the Paris Marathon and one of the biggest in the world should be amongst the World Majors, especially as 42 per cent of the entries hail from overseas, with as many as 150 nationalities taking part. Though not being classed as a Major it's had incredible success over the past 40 years. After all, this is a marathon through the most beautiful city in the world! Who can fail to hum, 'I Love Paris' whilst passing the finish line at the Arc de Triomphe?

17 CAYMAN ISLANDS MARATHON

Grand Cayman, Cayman Islands   Road   December   www.caymanislandsmarathon.com

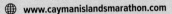

DISTANCE

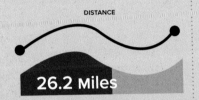

26.2 Miles

HR **MIN** **SEC**

`0 2` `3 6` `2 3`

FASTEST TIME (KNOWN)

`0 3` `0 8` `5 0`

TOBIAS' FINISHING TIME

86% COMPLETION RATE

Is there any running enthusiast who, given the chance, would refuse an invitation to a marathon on a warm, sunlit island in the middle of December? And if, as an added bonus, this island, with its glorious white sandy beaches, would also make a perfect holiday or honeymoon destination, well, surely there can only be one response.

Happily, the Intertrust Cayman Islands Marathon caters for all tastes, abilities and preferences. The race is run on Grand Cayman, the largest of the three Caribbean islands that are still part of the British Overseas Territory. The annual marathon is one of the big events of the year and some 1,200 locals take part, as well as running enthusiasts from around the globe.

With three possible choices – a relay marathon, half marathon or a full 26.2 miles, the course is not just beautiful, but for those who don't always relish ascents and descents and/or are looking for a PB, it's primarily flat.

The race begins, whatever distance you might have chosen, in the capital, George Town, at 5 o'clock in the morning. In order to be at the start line on time, this meant a sharp 3.30 a.m. wake-up by the hotel alarm service which, it must be honest, was a bit of a shock to the system as we'd already gone into relaxed mode. However, at the start line were a thousand competitors milling about with an air of indisputable excitement. To add to the throng were hundreds of well-wishers – friends and family of the island competitors – who'd also risen in the small hours to lend their support. Enthusiastic support, I should add, that they warmly extended to all the foreign visitors. More akin to a social night with a running club, it was a great beginning to the race.

Being a two-loop course, I set off with my usual eagerness to get into the lead pack, but I soon discovered exactly why this race had started before dawn. The temperature began to rise swiftly and I soon found that a slight

Grand Cayman from the air.

OPPOSITE: Showing off our new finisher medals.

RIGHT: Sometimes, it's tempting to veer off course and dive into the beautiful sea.

The other consolation was the exceptionally good aid stations. Always the food and drink was fantastic and so was the welcome as you stopped at each one, situated every two miles. The runners had been asked to vote for the best aid station, so some put out all the stops to impress by wearing every kind of fancy dress. This, and the cheering crowds by now lining the route, kept me going. I must admit I was extremely glad that the course was indeed a flat one as I'm not sure I would have relished too many hills.

As I completed the half marathon first loop, I was sitting comfortably in second position, with first being some distance away. But then the wheels fell off and despite my best efforts, I gradually slipped into third position, which I clung onto despite the fact that my legs were slowing down to a strange, piston-like movement made not so much for speed as sheer endurance. Perhaps I'd overestimated matters by taking on my third marathon in what now seemed like five very short weeks and my body was making its protest known.

I'm not usually one for dramatic finishes but as I crossed the line, all I could do was collapse into a nearby chair, where I received one of the largest and heaviest medals I've ever known. It was an effort simply to put it around my neck. But I did have just enough strength to wander over with my wife Zayne to the very inviting white sandy beach and its warm, refreshing waters. The beauty of the island, the enthusiastic welcome from the people and the delights of an escape to sunshine in chilly December make this a race to enjoy wholeheartedly. Before it began, one British runner told me he'd already done it six times. As we strolled back along Seven Mile Beach, I understood why – but perhaps next time I'll do the relay!

touch of jet lag combined with the heat (it was in the late twenties, even at 5 a.m.) was slowing me down. In fact, I had a moment or two when I wished I'd opted, like my sensible wife, for the half marathon. But there were several consolations, the first being that as the light and heat grew stronger, there was the lure of the pristine white beaches that I could glimpse in the near distance. 'Later,' I kept telling myself, 'later I'll be able to go there. Later, I can swim in those aqua-blue waters.' For now, it was a question of slogging on and making sure I wasn't overtaken by too many people.

Top tips

- Although it's December, don't underestimate the heat: even first thing in the morning it can be as hot as 30°C!
- Make a holiday (or even a honeymoon) out of it – there's so much to see and do

SUCKER FOR PUNISHMENT

18

SUCKER FOR PUNISHMENT

NEW YORK CITY MARATHON

New York, USA   Road   269m   November www.tcsnycmarathon.org

DISTANCE

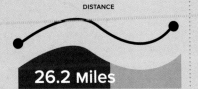

26.2 Miles

HR	MIN	SEC
0 2	0 5	0 5

FASTEST TIME (KNOWN)

| 0 2 | 5 7 | 2 3 |

TOBIAS' FINISHING TIME

99% COMPLETION RATE

Upon arrival in Staten Island, the start area of the New York City Marathon, you might be forgiven for thinking you've just reached a refugee camp. Everywhere you look, runners are wrapped up in old tracksuit tops, unwanted onesies given by doting grandparents, discarded space blankets, old duvets and sleeping bags that may have seen better days. Some have even brought pieces of cardboard to sit on. And nearly everyone has taken advantage of the free fleece hats being distributed, even if they do make you look like the court jester!

Doing a race like the New York City Marathon – the biggest marathon in the world – isn't just a tick in the box: it's an entire experience. The excitement of visiting the Big Apple, a place where limos are as common as bicycles, yellow taxis impatiently dart about the place, steam comes out of manhole covers and the Empire State Building soars high over the city. Then there's Central Park, the Statue of Liberty, and the list goes on.

Big city road marathons, by their very nature, tend to be relatively fast and flat. And a World Marathon Major such as New York City, first held in 1970, shouldn't be any different except with the race taking place in November, there are three major variables that might hinder efforts to beat your PB: bridges, wind and chilly temperatures. This may not sound particularly alarming, but believe me, for the 50,000-odd people running beside me in the 2014 edition

of New York, they will factor high on their 'How did the race go?' response.

But when you're picking up your race number at the expo several days earlier, you're not thinking about any of this. Mostly, you're simply revelling in the fact that for the space of a weekend in November, New York is a city of runners. And you can't fail to spot them, as nearly every single one will have purchased some form of Asics-sponsored New York Marathon memento.

Once you hear the sound of the canon, you know you're away and sweaters, onesies and old T-shirts are discarded with vigour. I'd been warned about not going off too hard in the first six or so miles, but luckily that wasn't a problem. As soon as we hit the mile-long Verrazano-Narrows Bridge, I might as well have been in a wind tunnel, the 40mp/h headwind smashing into us like water from a dam. Even drafting behind some of the bigger runners did little to shelter me from the elements, the wind tearing through my singlet like sand through one's hands.

Just as the Comrades Marathon (see also page 130) is defined by its Five Hills, the New York City Marathon is all about the five boroughs of Staten Island, The Bronx, Brooklyn, Queens and Manhattan – and you'll pass through every one. For the first timer in New York it's fascinating to see the different architecture that identifies the borough you're running through. But most noticeable is the support – it's as though each borough is trying to outdo the other. I particularly liked the

Near the start, the first bridge you'll cross is the Verrazano-Narrows Bridge.

welcome we got from The Bronx, with one placard reading: 'Welcome to The Bronx. Now get the hell out of here!'

As I've mentioned, the bridges play an important part in the race. Where some might argue they're a perfect opportunity to see the city in a different perspective, others would argue (and I'm in their camp on this one) that they represent an uphill struggle. The worst was Queensboro Bridge – a 2.27km long structure connecting Long Island City with Manhattan. By the time I reached Manhattan, the final borough, I could have kissed the ground with joy – so grateful was I to be off the bridge at last!

After this, there's just the wind tunnel of Fifth Avenue to contend with before you finally reach the sheltered enclave of Central Park – paradise compared to what I'd just been through. Twisting and turning my way through the park towards the finish, I felt as though I was on a movie set, my memory jogged by all the famous scenes filmed in those 843 leafy acres. All the fanfare and bravado about running the world biggest marathon, it's totally worth it!

Top tips

- Take the pre-arranged transportation to the start; it's much easier than public transport
- Being in November, take plenty of discardable warm layers for the start, as well as potentially a hat for the race itself

OPPOSITE: The route takes you along 5th Avenue, through the heart of Manhattan.

BELOW: Runners make their way across Queensboro Bridge – the longest on the course.

19 QUEENSTOWN INTERNATIONAL MARATHON

Queenstown, New Zealand   Trail, road   440m   12 November   www.queenstown-marathon.co.nz

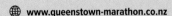

DISTANCE

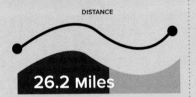

26.2 Miles

HR	MIN	SEC
0 2	3 3	4 1

FASTEST TIME (KNOWN)

| 0 2 | 5 9 | 0 9 |

TOBIAS' FINISHING TIME

99%
COMPLETION
RATE

If you've ever harboured a desire to visit New Zealand, then it's very likely you've heard of Queenstown. For mountain sports enthusiasts in the Southern Hemisphere, this is their Valhalla. The town practically oozes a sense of adventure, as like-minded souls gather like moths to a flame to hike, trail run, cycle, mountain bike, climb, kayak, bungee jump, paraglide or simply enjoy any of the other myriad sporting options on offer. But up until November 2014, the town lacked one thing: a marathon to call its own. Of course there were plenty of races up in the mountains that would take you up hill and down dale, but nothing that actually took place in the immediate vicinity of Queenstown itself.

So when I heard about the inaugural Air New Zealand Queenstown International Marathon, a race that would be 'flat out beautiful' on 70 per cent trail and the remainder on tarmac, I signed up immediately – even though it was 11,000 miles on the other side of the world. Add to the fact that it takes place at the end of November, which is the start of the summer down under, and I was well up for a bit of sun. For me, this was a chance to race a fast trail marathon in one of the most iconic towns in the Southern Hemisphere.

With the race being sponsored by Air New Zealand, the organisers, Lagardère Unlimited, were very much hoping to attract runners not just from outside of Queenstown but from overseas as well. Clearly, Lagardère, who also look after the ITU World Triathlon Championship Series, did something right, because the race not only sold out in the first year alone, months before cut off, but exceeded their five-year targets, attracting a staggering 6,000 runners across the various distances.

In the world of marathons this race is just a baby, but it's already made a name for itself as one to add to your bucket list.

Being a point-to-point course, shuttle buses take you from Queenstown centre to the start at the Millbrook Resort, one of New Zealand's most prestigious golf courses. It was a useful opportunity to see many of the sights we'd pass along parts of the route, including a few of the cheeky hills that drew a couple of expletives from runners on the bus. I also noted with dread the ominous clouds heading our way, as though from a scene in *Lord of the Rings*, which incidentally was filmed in the area.

ABOVE: Even in poor weather, the scenery around Queenstown is breathtaking.

BELOW: The Crown and Remarkable mountain ranges are ever present in the background.

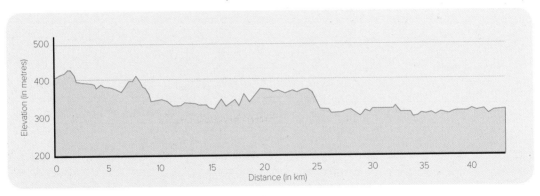

The race bills itself as a 'mainly flat, fast course with a few undulations to keep it interesting' – 'undulations' being the operative word. Of course, surrounded by the Crown and Remarkable mountain ranges, it's no surprise to see the odd hill or two. But looking at the course profile, it seems deceptively flat to the point of being downhill. The thing is – it isn't. These 'undulations' are short and sharp hills. After a while, they'll wind you like a blow to the stomach combined with mega loss of leg power.

Every time you go up and down one of them, you feel not just your strength ebbing away but as is so important in most marathons, the essential ability to keep a steady pace.

The rain had started to ease up a little and the cloud cover lifted at times, allowing us to see spectacular views. Passing through the gold rush village of Arrowtown, with its quaint shops, cafés and hotels, all styled as if still

BELOW: Lake Hayes.

in the nineteenth century, we headed down towards Lake Hayes and its purpose-built trails.

The aid stations were spaced every seven or so kilometres, appearing just when you needed them most. But as soon as I thought the rain had lifted, it then came down with a vengeance, making me glad I was wearing trail shoes as the ground was getting slippery. I was not just soaking in the rain, but also the stunning scenery. New Zealand really is a magical country and I found myself constantly looking over my shoulder, not to see the runners behind me but the views of the mountains.

BELOW: Runners passing through Arrowtown, a former gold-mining town from the nineteenth century

ABOVE: The course takes you along the Lake Hayes lakeside trail.

Although there's only one long 6km stretch of tarmac, which I admit I was glad to see the back of, it's the sort of trail running you can only dream of in a race. Sure, it is lumpy in places, but this added another element to an already fantastic race. Running the final 10km along the banks of the glacial-fed Lake Wakatipu, the third-largest lake in New Zealand and one of the few lakes in the world to have a tide, I fell in love with Queenstown. It offers everything that an outdoor enthusiast could want – including an awesome marathon!

Top tips

- Normal road trainers are fine, unless there's a chance of rain
- Don't hesitate too long about entering as it will sell out relatively quickly

SUCKER FOR PUNISHMENT

20 LE MARATHON DU MÉDOC

Médoc Region, France   Trail: mix of vineyards and road   September www.marathondumedoc.com

DISTANCE

26.2 Miles

HR	MIN	SEC
0 2	2 8	4 1

FASTEST TIME (KNOWN) CUT-OFF: 6:30

0 5 0 1 0 0

TOBIAS' FINISHING TIME

90% COMPLETION RATE

Exhausted but happy, there's a celebratory atmosphere on the finishing straight.

'Glass of wine, sir?' *Don't mind if I do!* 'Ice cream?' *Oh yes, please!* 'Champagne with that?' *Oh all right, if you insist.* Very few marathons stipulate you run in fancy dress, whilst encouraging you to enjoy wine, foie gras, cheese, steak, oysters, ice cream and champagne en route. But the Marathon du Médoc isn't just any marathon. In fact, Le Médoc, which was founded in 1984, calls itself the '*Marathon le plus long du monde*' – for the simple reason that rather than chasing Personal Bests, you're aiming to finish in the longest time possible just before the cut-off. Because this is one race where you want to get value for money, especially with 23 wine stops to sample.

Now, it's fair to say that there are certain rules about marathon running:

1. Never try anything new on race day. Now I have to admit the first time I ran the Médoc I did so in full Roman General costume, one my helpful girlfriend (now wife) Zayne had unwittingly cut so high

Wine isn't what you'd normally expect at a marathon aid station, but luckily water is also on hand.

it required a pair of shorts to maintain my modesty. I didn't fancy trotting down Wandsworth High Street in that! Make sure you try your costume out before the race.

2. Avoid alcohol the night before. So, would a couple of glasses of champagne and a glass of wine consumed at a party the previous evening have any noticeable effect? Not the best plan, as I discovered, but to each his own.

3. Avoid alcohol during the race itself. Now this can be tricky but they do serve water along with the Château Lafite.

4. Don't stop too often or you'll find it hard to get going again. How long is 'not too long'? Sampling some of the best claret in the world can take a minute or two!

5. Never eat anything you've not tested out in training. In theory, this is an excellent idea but with foie gras, mussels, pâté, entrecôte and even an ice cream or two on offer, it requires a certain degree of willpower and the ability to say, '*Non, merci beaucoup*,' in your most polite French.

6. Be sure to carbo load in the 24 hours leading up to the race. Tick! But it's perhaps wisest if those carbs don't include a generous portion or two of gourmet patisserie.

Well, if there's one thing for certain, it's likely you're going to break every single one of those rules – something I discovered on the two occasions I've run this race.

The start is what the French might refer to as '*un spectacle*' – professional dancers, music, masses of confetti in the air … it's amazing! Once the race was underway, we were full of enthusiasm, gladly toasting each other's

good health whilst commenting on on how much fun we were having. With temperatures reaching around 40°C, by mile 18 we hit a veritable wall of pain, thanks to running out of carbohydrates, severe dehydration and almighty hangovers. Suddenly, we were less interested in the wine and more so in the water. But Zayne and I loved the race so much, we returned two years later, when we ran with our guests before getting married at the end.

Aside from the joys of sampling Château Lafite Rothschild, Pichon Longueville and

Château Grand Puy La-Coste, this race is all about fancy dress. In fact, you're actively discouraged from wearing any form of Lycra that might make you look like a runner. Depending on the chosen theme for that year, you'll find a cornucopia of alarming outfits that leave nothing to the imagination, but will have you giggling away like school kids. This also means there's a high likelihood of chaffage in parts you'd rather not talk about in public.

Not everyone, though, is out to enjoy themselves as much as we were. The various châteaux contributing the wine you'll find en route also enter teams, with much importance being laid on gathering the quickest runners they can find. The winner blasts a trail through the course, finishing in 2:30, whilst 90 per cent of the field aim to finish at the 6 hours 30 cut-off.

By the time we collapsed over the finish line, looking like we'd just spent 40 days and nights in the desert, we were rewarded with a rose, a bottle of wine, a bag and a medal before we proceeded to the finishers' tent, where we were further rewarded with enough food and drink to feed an army.

A word of caution: if you like the sound of this race, be sure to keep an eye out on when entries open, as they sell out immediately.

Top tips

- Book your accommodation and flights early on
- Although the 6 hours 30 cut-off sounds generous, limit your time at the wine stops

Even after 26.2 miles, you'll never tire of seeing the rolling vineyards of this beautiful region.

21 SNOWDONIA MARATHON ERYRI

 Snowdonia, Wales   Road and trail   851m   12 October   www.snowdoniamarathon.co.uk

DISTANCE

26.2 Miles

HR	MIN	SEC
0 2	3 5	4 0

FASTEST TIME (2012)

0 3 1 0 0 3

TOBIAS' FINISHING TIME

97% COMPLETION RATE

First established in 1982, the Brooks Snowdonia Marathon Eryri has built a reputation for being one of the most scenic road marathons in the UK, and somewhat ironically, one of the toughest too. Indeed, if you're thinking this would be a good place to get a PB, think again. But if you want to run an iconic marathon around the highest mountain in Wales, then this is it.

Having registered at the curiously named Electric Mountain, you'll then make your way to the start, just outside of Llanberis. It's a bit of a walk and a chance to soak in what's in store. With the race being held in the Snowdonia National Park, the weather can be particularly fickle, especially at the end of October, when sunshine is the exception rather than the rule. In fact, I was warned that if it wasn't raining, I'd be lucky. So be prepared to brace yourself for what could be a wet, cold and windy day. But that doesn't seem to put anyone off and

certainly not any of the UK's elite mountain and marathon runners, from Martin Cox and Rob Samuel to ultra supremo Lizzy Hawker.

Once you reach the start line, situated on the banks of Llyn Peris, you can't fail to notice the palpable level of excitement in the air. It's the same feeling you get when you're about to do something quite difficult, yet achievable. Maybe that's the magical quality of Snowdonia. The first few miles are reasonably flat but they are followed by a considerable 1,100ft climb out of Llanberis up to Pen-y-Pass. As you grind your way up in altitude, there's the chance to stare in awe at The Glyders on the left and the Snowdon massif on the right, complete with majestic waterfalls dripping off the mountainside.

Once on the other side, the descent down the Pass towards Pen-y-Gwryd was a bit of a shock to my quads, which had been working hard to

The Llanberis Pass — flanked by the Glyderau and Snowdon massif.

ABOVE: The race starts with an uphill slog along Llanberis Pass.

OPPOSITE: Most of the route is on road, but there are a few trail sections.

get me up Llanberis Pass. And then, around six miles in, we hung a sharp right at the bottom of the pass and hit the first bit of trail. Yes, just in case you're not aware, the Snowdonia Marathon isn't entirely on tarmac – which is a blessing to trail runners and a curse to roadies.

The stretch of trail is only two miles long, but my feet were grateful for the change of surface, although I did see a few runners wearing minimalist shoes wincing and cursing with pain whenever they stepped on a stone. I was simply grateful that we were going downhill, but not so abruptly that we were likely to get cramp. By the time I'd reached the halfway point I was beginning to feel pretty good. Even the two-mile long hill coming out of the pretty village of Beddgelert didn't feel so bad compared to the Pen-y-Pass.

After the second climb, I managed to build up my pace again, despite the lumpy and undulating nature of the course, largely because I was so busy chatting with another runner who I'd bumped into at the start. I even forgot to hit the proverbial 'Wall', normally around the 18–20 mile point. But that's because the organisers of the race were saving the 'Wall' for mile 22. It's at this point, at the entrance to Waunfawr, that

the ground starts to go up, progressively at first, but as you exit the village, it gets steeper and steeper for another two miles.

'Ah,' I thought to myself as my legs started to go into meltdown. 'This is where the true sting in the tail is.'

Reaching the summit, the road turned briefly to track, and I stumbled down the final brutal descent towards Llanberis and ultimately the finish line – which I reached in 3 hours 10 minutes – a full 27 minutes behind the winner, Rob Samuel.

There's no medal in this race, but a Snowdonia Marathon Eryri slate coaster from the nearby former quarry is awarded instead. I don't normally collect coasters, but I'd be tempted to do it again and create a set. This is one marathon it's worth coming back for.

Top tips

- Take your own energy gels as there aren't any on the course
- With there being a few trail sections, minimalist shoes aren't recommended

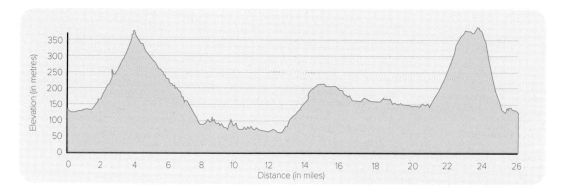

FISHERMAN'S FRIEND STRONGMAN RUN

📍 Nürburgring, Germany

⬜◻⬜ 18 obstacles per lap

〰〰 Road, trail and obstacles

📅 May

🌐 www.fishermansfriend.de/strongmanrun/en

DISTANCE

15 Miles (12KM PER LAP)

HR	MIN	SEC
0 1	4 4	0 0

FASTEST TIME (KNOWN)

| 0 2 | 1 0 | 0 0 |

TOBIAS' FINISHING TIME

79% COMPLETION RATE

Despite taking place in nine countries around Europe and attracting well over 50,000 entrants from 43 nations, there's a good chance you may not have heard of the Fisherman's Friend Strongman Run. That's because there isn't a UK edition, even though it's sponsored by a 150-year-old UK company that makes über-strong menthal lozenges.

Thanks to the power of the lozenge, the Strongman Run, or to use its nickname, 'Green Hell', has become one of the most popular obstacle courses outside the UK. The first edition of the race took place in 2007 on a military training ground in Munster, Germany, before moving several years later to its current location at the Nürburgring.

As if running a half-marathon obstacle course isn't difficult enough, the night before the race the organisers lay on a massive party, where people dance and drink as though there's no tomorrow. Come the morning, any groggy heads are quickly knocked into touch the moment you stand in the starting pen.

As with most obstacle races, you can either choose to run with friends and take the 'completer' attitude, joining the throngs of Spartans, Smurfs and Supermen. Or you can run it alone, gunning for a position. Either option works well with this race. But unlike rival races with multiple waves throughout the day, the Strongman Run has just one, making it the biggest obstacle race in the world. And if you want to be a contender, then you need to ensure you are in the Elite starting pen, as it takes up to 20 minutes for all 13,500 contenders to cross the start line.

The race is essentially two laps of the world-famous Nürburgring motorsports complex, totalling about 24km and 18 obstacles per lap. It also gains about 900m in height – something that I wasn't personally aware of before the race – taking small detours off the track and

up nearby hills. It's got everything you could possibly want – deep mud pits, water holes, hurdles to clamber over, ice-filled ponds, slippery and steep water slides, climbing nets, bales of straw, a slimy basin and the pièce de résistance, the Eiffel – a gargantuan tower you need to climb over.

Listening to the ever-popular AC/DC blast out on loud speakers, it's impossible not to get psyched up for this event. And by the time the starting piston goes, you'll be biting on the bit, raring to go. Of course, being on a racing circuit, especially one as ferocious as the Nürburgring, famous for its tight bends that have thrown many a racing driver into the gravel traps, you'll be sprinting off the starting grid as though your life depended upon it. However, strategically

The Strongman Run is not just a race – but a chance to have fun (and for some, a decent bath).

placed giant bales of hay do an excellent job of slowing you down and reminding you there's still a long way to go.

As you work your way through the course, becoming increasingly wet, muddy and exhausted, it becomes harder to keep the momentum, especially when leopard crawling through cages whilst trying to dodge dangling electric wires that occasionally brush your face, causing you to emit the odd swear word. But it's not all 'hard' work, as some of the obstacles, believe it or not, are sheer pleasure – in particular the enormous water-slide that will have you squealing with delight.

Top tips:

- If you want to do well, make sure you're in the Elite wave
- Consider taking fingerless gloves to help with the rope climbs

More mud, more gravel traps – which are just as good at slowing down runners as racing cars – lead you to perhaps the most sadistic of Dr Evil's dastardly obstacles: Mount Neverest. A one-mile uphill stretch, littered with car tyres, straw bales and anything else the good Doctor could find, it feels as if it could literally go on for ever.

Just when you think you can't take any more, convinced you've done most of the obstacles, they produce more. One of my favourites was 'Tropic Hell Island' – a 40m long, 2m deep pool, which forces almost everyone but the tallest to swim it. But it's a short-lived reprieve as this is simply to get you wet for 'Shock Norris' – a tyre obstacle with more electric wires dangling down that you seriously need to avoid. A word of caution: if you do slip on a tyre, don't grab hold of the electric cords, as I did. It's enough of a shock to bring Frankenstein's monster back to life! And a shock is exactly what you need when you start the second lap. Eventually the finish line looms, but not before they make you clamber over 3,000 car tyres, several large transport containers and an enormous cargo net.

Atmosphere, incredible camaraderie, the party, the quality of the obstacles, an iconic racetrack and a lifetime's supply of lozenges … the Strongman Run has got it all!

Not your average cargo net to clamber over.

23 SPARTAN RACE

UK, USA and worldwide | Cross-country | 30–35 | 5,000ft

 November

spartanraceuk.uk

DISTANCE

12–14 Miles

HR	MIN	SEC
01	58	00

FASTEST TIME (KNOWN)

| 02 | 27 | 00 |

TOBIAS' FINISHING TIME

99% COMPLETION RATE

Face down on the ground, my arms are wobbling as I gear myself up to finish my last burpee. 'Why on earth,' I ask myself, 'did choose to do The Beast as my introduction to the Spartan Race series?'

Some weeks earlier, I had perhaps wisely completed a Spartan training camp with Wild Forest Gym in Essex, involving a great deal of scrambling around on hands and feet, precariously hanging off ropes, climbing 6ft walls, leaping between sticks and wading through ice-cold bogs – all whilst carrying a 6ft telegraph pole. I was somewhat sceptical as to how useful this would be – after all, I'd done plenty of other obstacle course races – but as I picked myself up off the ground and gingerly continued on to the next obstacle, everything started to make sense. The Spartan Beast was unlike anything I'd done before. In fact, I'd argue it was harder than any other obstacle course race – and I've done most of them: 2,500 people in exceptionally muddy fields and woodland, 30–35 obstacles and 5,000ft of ascent before you're finally allowed to chew on that ever so satisfying burger at the finish and call yourself a Spartan.

The Spartan Race series is divided into three distances – the Sprint (5K), Super (13K) and Beast (21K) – the main difference being the distance and naturally the number of obstacles. Many people enter the series to earn the coveted Trifecta Medal, which is awarded to those who complete each distance in one year. Others are OCR junkies who tour the country, bouncing from one obstacle race to the next in a blur of mud and barbed wire. And of course, many are simply there for the challenge of jumping over 9ft walls and scrambling under barbed wire, all in the name of fun.

But where Tough Mudder is all about teamwork, the Spartan Race is what it says on the tin: a race. And one you do on your own. However, don't worry, it's not all about brawn and muscle. You've also got to keep the grey matter on high alert, as some of the obstacles are of a cerebral nature, requiring you to do simple sums or remember a sequence of numbers that if you get wrong, will have you doing 30 punishment burpees – much harder than any obstacle!

On the final stretch, only a 15ft rope climb and a couple of spartan warriors separate you from the finish.

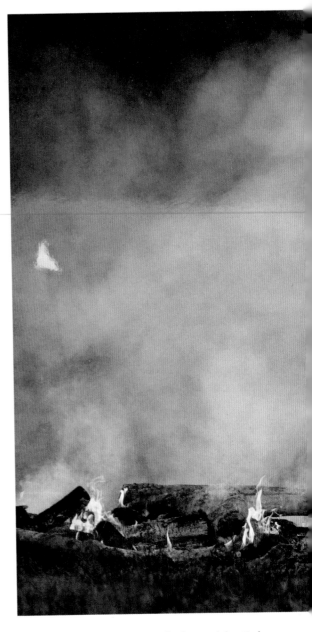

From the moment you're standing on the start line, where a man dressed as a Spartan gives a rousing speech similar to that from the film 300, right through to the finish, this is one massive endorphin rush. However, if you harbour any desire to do well in this race and be able to call yourself a Spartan champion, then you need to be in the first 'elite' wave of the day. Simply because if you don't, not only are you running on an ever-increasing quagmire of a course, but you'll also have to pass several hundred people who are not in such a hurry.

Over several hours I threw spears, pulled car tyres, carried logs, flipped tractor tyres, did mathematics and completed a host of other fun, yet challenging obstacles. The training I'd done with Wild Forest Gym was paying off. Sadly, I'd neglected to do any upper body training, which resulted in me falling off the monkey bars into the murky depths of a pool of water. As if that's not punishment enough, I then had to do 30 burpees.

As I approached the finish, I was ready to fall into a mud-splattered heap. But not before I had clambered over a 9ft wall, carried a 30kg atlas stone, banged out some press-ups, climbed up a 15ft-high rope and barged my way past a set of gladiators with giant candy-floss sticks. Only then did I finish, 2 hours and 27 minutes after I'd started. And only then could I rightly call myself a Spartan.

Don't let a little fire slow you down!

SUCKER FOR PUNISHMENT

24 TOUGH GUY

📍 Wolverhampton, UK   〰 Cross-country   ◻◻◻ 200+   📅 January   🌐 www.toughguy.co.uk

DISTANCE

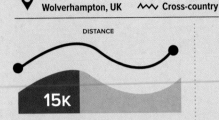

15K

HR	MIN	SEC
0 1	3 8	0 5

FASTEST TIME (KNOWN)

0 3 0 1 5 0

TOBIAS' FINISHING TIME

80%
COMPLETION
RATE

If you've ever wondered where the trend for subjecting oneself to electric-shock therapy whilst leopard crawling through mud before immersing oneself in ice-cold water, climbing over multiple 12ft walls and jumping over a fire pit came from, then you need to head to the outskirts of Wolverhampton at the end of January to track down an eccentric character named Billy Watson, AKA Mr Mouse.

Thanks to Mr Mouse we have the plethora of obstacle-course races, mud runs and the like. And it all began in January 1987 with a race called Tough Guy – one that's still going strong today and can rightly lay claim to being, 'The original and toughest test of its kind anywhere in the world'. Inspired by his military service with the British Army and the Grenadier Guards, Mr Mouse decided to replicate the obstacle courses where soldiers train, creating one where, 'Your fear of heights, tight spaces, fire, water and electricity will be tested to the max and everyone bar the very toughest will be beaten!' Fighting words indeed!

My first encounter with this iconic race happened in 2004. I was not long out of

Sandhurst and keen to put my military training to the test. Upon hearing about Tough Guy, a group of my fellow officers and I entered, thinking this would be a piece of cake. After all, having just attended the finest military academy in the world, how 'tough' could Tough Guy really be? It turned out we were in for a bit of a surprise.

The modern-day premise of Tough Guy is to 'Test oneself, on every discipline in life, in one day'. And if you're going to complete this course containing over 200 manmade obstacles, you'll need to draw on, 'Every last ounce of mental and physical strength' – words I might once have sniggered at, but having done it, now respect.

The race starts around 11 a.m., signalled by a canon shot – which seems entirely appropriate, given the setting. Sadly, being newbie Tough Guys, we started right at the back, where like a scene out of the film *Braveheart*, I found myself running alongside hoards of the most

No obstacle course race is complete without cargo ropes. However, swinging from them is quite difficult.

ABOVE: How not to jump over burning hay and into a bog.

OPPOSITE: Tough Guy is all about facing your fears and getting dirty.

extraordinary dressed competitors ranging from Roman soldiers to knights in shining armour. Some teams try to make their lives even more difficult by carrying a giant crucifix or in some cases, a canon. But when you see Mr Mouse's outfit, it all makes sense!

The first half of the race is more like a cross-country run interspersed with muddy obstacles, electric fences, trenches, scrambling under cargo nets, jumping over log trees and doing hill reps up and down the 'Rabbit Hill Dead Leg Slalom'. By the time I'd done all of this, I was actually looking forward to the aptly named 'Killing Fields' that follow.

Indeed, it is this part that makes Tough Guy stand out from many of the other races of its kind in that the obstacles are a permanent all-year round fixture. What's more, they're all manmade! Clearly, Mr Mouse is a dab hand with a chainsaw and digger. The only way to describe them is to imagine the set design of *Mad Max* merged with WaterWorld: grotesque, gigantic wooden structures that look like instruments of torture. Which is exactly what they are when you see the muddied bodies of men and women dripping off them like rats in a sewer. But the true torture lies in battle against any of the multitude of phobias you might be forgiven for having. If you've got a fear of tight spaces, then the Vietcong tunnels will be your worst nightmare. These are large sewage pipes, some of which are blocked, so you need to choose the right one if you don't want to get stuck.

If you're afraid of drowning, then you'll probably want to avoid the pitch-black underwater tunnels and of course being January, so cold your heart will beat faster than a hunted deer. They're my idea of hell.

So, you have a fear of heights? Well, you'll quickly have to get over it, whether that be

walking the plank, climbing the 8m high Tiger or tackling the even taller 10m high Behemoth comprised of tree-top ropes in between telegraph poles.

But this is exactly why you enter Tough Guy. It's about dressing up in a ridiculous outfit, scaring yourself witless, getting covered in mud and pushing your body to the very limits of what you thought possible in the world's original obstacle course race. But one thing's for certain: apart from those underwater moments, you'll be grinning the whole way round. Especially when you're handed the horse brass finisher's medal – perhaps the coolest medal you'll ever receive!

Top tips:

- Try to wear fast-wicking clothes even if it's fancy dress
- Take discardable gloves – you'll appreciate them on the rope sections or simply to avoid splinters
- Bring the gnarliest trainers with the most grip you can find!

The founder, Mr Mouse, was inspired by his time in the military – thus the use of lots of barbed wire!

25

SUCKER FOR PUNISHMENT

RACE TO THE STONES

The Ridgeway, UK · ∿∿ Trail · 702m · 📅 July · 🌐 www.racetothestones.com

DISTANCE

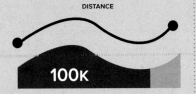

100k

	HR	MIN	SEC
	0 8	2 0	3 0

FASTEST TIME (KNOWN)

1 0 4 4 0 0

TOBIAS' FINISHING TIME

80%
COMPLETION RATE

The Ridgeway is Britain's oldest road.

If you could design a race to offer almost everything a runner could ask for, then the Dixon Carphone Race to the Stones could well be the one. Only an hour's journey from London, it follows the oldest road in Britain and one of the UK's most beautiful national trails. Best of all, you can choose to walk it, run it, complete it in a single day or even spread it out over two days. All in all, it's one of the most accessible ultra-marathons in the UK.

Indeed, until recently ultra-marathons in the UK had never reached the scale one might expect of a European event, such as the Ultra-Trail du Mont-Blanc or Transvulcania (see also pages 188 and 228). But the Race to the Stones is about to change all that. Not only is it now the UK's largest ultra-marathon, with well over 2,000 people signing up, it's also trying to

This incredible field is one of the race's most memorable features.

reset the gender balance with almost half the entrants being female

'More is in You' is the mantra of the organisers, Threshold Sports, and with Race to the Stones they're aiming not only to create an exceptional event but also an experience.

The course follows the Ridgeway, a route that lays claim to being the oldest road in Britain. For 10,000 years, from Neolithic man to Saxon and Roman invaders, devout pilgrims to working farmers, this ancient trackway has carried the footprints of thousands of our ancestors. Running it is like being carried on a conveyor belt through history. You'll see the great stones of Wayland's Smithy, the Neolithic long barrow that served as a tomb for chieftain's families, pass along the tree-lined track of Grim's Ditch, offering welcome shade on a sweltering day and in the distance catch glimpses of the enormous and mysterious Uffington White Horse, etched into the ground and filled with crushed white chalk. Even Saint George is part of this ancient route, as nearby Dragon's Hill is alleged to be the site where he slayed his dragon.

Once stretching 250 miles from the Dorset coast through to The Wash on the north coast, nowadays it's a mere 86 miles. But Race to the Stones begins near Lewknor, in Oxfordshire and follows the Ridgeway's final 60-odd miles. And as the name suggests, you're racing to Avebury Stones, the largest stone circle in Europe. But be aware that you'll also have to doubleback on yourself and finish just around the corner, so make sure you keep a bit in the tank for the final few kilometres.

A fully supported event, Threshold Sports still insist you bring a few mandatory items, just in case, such as a spare long-sleeved top, waterproof jacket, hat and gloves – which felt somewhat precautionary in the inaugural race, as it happened to be the hottest day of the year. But as British weather is notoriously unreliable, it's best to cover all options. In fact, despite having ploughed through the Sahara sands, I must admit the roasting sun on the Ridgeway that Saturday, in July 2013, certainly slowed me down. However, in retrospect, I'm grateful that the all too frequent pauses at the excellent aid stations every 10km, offering delicious and tempting things to eat, gave me the chance to mop my brow and take deep breaths – and enjoy a greater appreciation of this extraordinary route.

For those choosing to spread the race over two days, there's an optional overnight camp, where you're able to put your feet up and enjoy an excellent dinner, a good night's rest

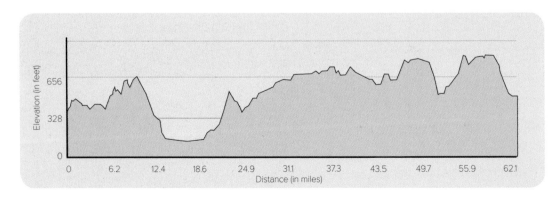

in the tents provided and a hearty breakfast, before setting out for the final 50km. Even better, Threshold will carry your overnight kit for you.

Despite the boiling heat of the inaugural race day, I finally crossed the finish line a little later than I'd have liked in 10 hours 44 and collapsed at last in a wheezing, gasping and perspiring heap. But whatever distance or time span you choose, there's one thing you're guaranteed to discover: the Ridgeway is truly one of the most beautiful and inspiring trails in England. Finally, when you wander over to Avebury, the only stone circle in the world to contain a working pub and a chapel, you'll not know whether to seek redemption or quench your thirst with a pint.

Top tips

- Take a high-factor sun cream — there's very little shade on the path
- Use the aid stations, spaced every 10km, to break up the distance into manageable chunks
- Although road shoes are fine, trail shoes are advisable if it's wet. They have bigger lugs and better grip

Being on a ridgeline, there's no shelter from the sun.

SUCKER FOR PUNISHMENT

MAN VS HORSE
MARATHON

📍 **Powys, Wales**　〰 **Trail and fell**　🪜 **1,200m**　📅 **June**　🌐 **www.green-events.co.uk**

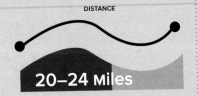

DISTANCE

20–24 Miles

HR　MIN　SEC

0 2 3 0 0 0

FASTEST TIME (2015)

0 3 3 0 0 0

TOBIAS' FINISHING TIME (2013 for 24 MILES)

99%
COMPLETION
RATE

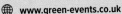

In a race that's called Man vs Horse, I shouldn't have been surprised to see a rider pass me. Nevertheless it's slightly unnerving hearing a horse bound up behind you, the rhythmic clip-clop of hooves on trail, the sound of it chewing on the bit, nostrils flared as it flexes its head. Determined not to be trampled upon, I move to the side of the trail, where the cheery rider (who goes on to win the race) shouts a thank you before disappearing into the distance. His horse gives a swoosh of his tale as if to say, 'Adieu, runner'.

For the past 35-plus years, man has battled against horse in this annual Man vs Horse Marathon across the challenging terrain of Powys, mid-Wales, complete with 4,000ft of climbing, heather, fell, streams, boggy trails, crags and technical descents. One of the earliest events in the World Alternative Games, it has gained a worldwide reputation for its quirky rules and the toughness of the course.

Like so many of the best ideas, this one was fuelled by a few drinks: 30-plus years ago, Gordon Green, landlord of the The Neuadd Arms Hotel in Llanwrtyd Wells, heard two of his patrons discussing the 'relative merits of men and horses running over mountainous terrain' over a beer. One of the men thought that in the right conditions and over a certain distance, 'man was equal to any horse'.

With the town already hosting the World Bogsnorkelling Championships, just one of many events in the Alternative Olympics, it was perfectly natural to put this theory to the test and so in 1980 the first Man vs Horse Marathon was held. Since then, the annual event has attracted hundreds of runners and riders, but it took a full 25 years before man finally had his way, when GB marathon runner Huw Lobb took

Although the runners have a head start, it's not long before a horse overtakes you.

When you hear the clippety-clop of a horse and rider behind you, it's normally a good idea to let them pass.

the overall win in 2004 by two minutes. In the process he claimed the prize money of £25,000 offered by bookmaker William Hill, which had been accumulating by £500 every year since the race started. However, this did not mark a winning streak and only once more has man triumphed over his four-legged rival when Florian Holzinger of Germany won the race in 2007.

Top tips

- If the idea of chasing a horse for 20-odd miles is too much, there is the three-person relay option
- It makes sense to give way to any horses trying to pass you

The event really begins the night before, with a pasta party at The Neuadd Arms Hotel. And with the race not starting until 11 a.m. and Llanwrtyd Wells being officially the world's smallest town, there's not much to do except drink, eat and afterwards, go to bed. Which if you're staying down the road at the campsite might be a restless night's sleep, thanks to the abundance of mosquitoes hovering nearby.

The next morning, I found myself back at the pub, standing with several hundred runners, including four-times Ironman World Champion Chrissie Wellington, all of us looking expectantly at the horses parading past. I was quietly relieved that they started 15 minutes after the runners, not only to avoid trampling on us but also to make sure we had a fighting

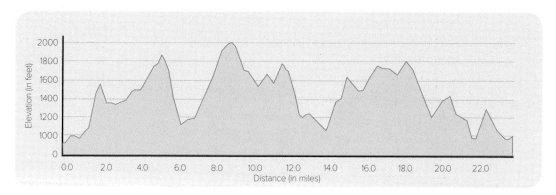

chance. Once the starting signal was given, we sprinted through the town as though the horses were truly just behind us. Unsurprisingly, our exuberance was short-lived when less than two miles into the race, we hit the first of many hills, before veering off-road and along streams, across bogs and up still more hills.

Despite being called a marathon, the course has changed quite a bit over the years and is now 'only' 20 miles, but you'll be jolly glad it's not any further! It took a full 45 minutes before the first rider overtook me and then more and more swiftly followed. Although it appears that on hot days horses fare less well as they're not so nimble as us humans when going downhill, neither the muggy and overcast weather nor the technical descents appeared to slow down the leading horses.

Rather than feel any need to speed up, it was mesmerising to watch these stunning animals go by, their riders wishing us luck as they rode on. In fact, the good humour of both riders and runners made this race feel very special. However, I wasn't just overtaken by horses but also the occasional human, when fresh-faced runners would replace weary ones. At first I was a little confused by where they'd come from, but then I discovered there was a three-leg relay option – which at certain points in the race, I'm sure one or two of the marathon runners wished they'd known about before entering.

As the miles ticked by and the horses overtook me, I was glad to see the end, near Victoria Wells, was within sight. With only a few more streams to cross and an uphill field at the end that sucked the life out of me, I was ready to collapse in a heap as I crossed the line in 3 hours 30 minutes, in 49th overall and 20th-placed human. This is a thoroughly enjoyable and exhausting event – and one guaranteed to increase your respect for the equine race.

In the history of the race, man has only beaten the horse twice.

27 RACE THE TRAIN

 Tywyn, Wales   Fields and footpaths   370m   August   www.racethetrain.com

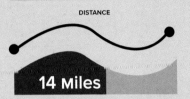

14 Miles

DISTANCE

HR	MIN	SEC
0 1	1 8	1 5

FASTEST TIME (KNOWN) MEN'S RECORD

| 0 1 | 3 1 | 4 1 |

TOBIAS' FINISHING TIME

CUT-OFF: 3:15
(768 PEOPLE ACHIEVED THAT IN 2014)

20%
COMPLETION
RATE
2013

If you stop for a moment to think of a few of the things you might race against – horses, camels, greyhounds and ostriches – a train may not come top of your list. The four-footed ones at least offer the possibility that you might succeed in beating them. But the train – hmm … how likely is that? However, for the small Welsh seaside town of Tywyn this is an annual event, where the 90-year-old steam train, who is the runner to beat, has been successful in challenging us two-legged creatures to a lively cross-country run since 1984.

As a dweller in a big city like London, all too often I've had to make a mad sprint for a train and once or twice leapt aboard as it sped off. So unsurprisingly this particular race caught my eye as one to add to the bucket list. Organised by the Rotary Club of Tywyn, the race is enjoyed not just by locals and not-so-local participants, but even runners from abroad. What's more, there's a jolly atmosphere built around this splendid old train, which in fact served as the inspiration for the much-loved children's books about Thomas the Tank Engine and is owned by the

Runners have around 1 hour and 47 minutes to beat the 100-year-old steam train.

narrow-gauge Talyllyn Railway, the world's first preserved nineteenth-century railway.

What makes this race particularly special is that family and friends can join you – not across the 14 miles of fields, rough pastures and muddy farm tracks that the runners must cross through – but in the comfort of fully appointed railway carriages.

The race starts at the main railway line bridge, just next to the Talyllyn Wharf railway station. Already there's an air of excitement as the whiff of smoke drifts towards us and a sharp whistle from the train announces it's ready for the challenge. Knowing that the train will take exactly 1 hour and 47 minutes to do the out-and-back journey, and with a cut-off for all runners of 3 hours and 15 minutes, if I was to beat the train then I needed to get a move on – especially with the sobering fact that generally speaking only 10 per cent of competitors manage to do this. Indeed, with a speed of 9–10mph, it might be difficult, if not impossible, to 'beat the train' whilst running up hill and down dale, but fortunately, it stops at several stations along the route to allow passengers to get on and off. And with a

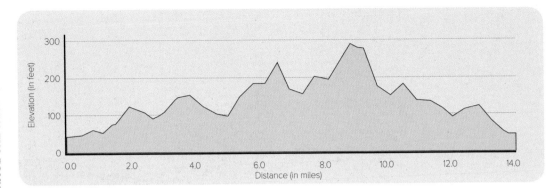

10-minute turnaround at Abergynolwyn, the 1,100 runners are in with a chance – well at least 10 of them anyway!

I'd no illusions that this would be an easy 14 miles but I hadn't factored in shooting down quite so many farm drives or thundering over pastures where tussocks of grass seemed designed to catch your toes. As I ran through the trees I could hear the impatient chuffing and chugging of the train and realised I needed to put on a further spurt. I got to the turnaround point in 43 minutes so I figured that unless I bonked horribly or I was struck by lightning, I was in with a chance of arriving back in Tywyn before the train. However, I hadn't quite bargained on the return leg of the race, which follows a different route. It was getting tougher by the second. Suddenly I found myself staring at an extremely steep hill – after all, this is Wales – but it wasn't just the sharp ascent. The trail abruptly grew narrower and narrower, demanding a keen sense of balance to avoid slithering and sliding down a treacherous slope. Now and again the train emerged and passengers leaned out of the windows to shout encouragement – I certainly needed it!

As the train disappeared, I could still hear it in the distance and seriously wondered for a moment or two if I was going to make it in time as I felt my legs already protesting about being pummelled and pushed over the uneven terrain. The rain was easing now and to my delight I managed to cross the finish line in 14th place, in 1:30:41 – a comfortable 17 minutes ahead of the train!

To celebrate the end of the race, and of course, the cheery awards ceremony, the organisers hold a big party in a marquee. This is a race where you can take your mates, your running club or your family, and turn a challenging cross-country run into a thoroughly entertaining weekend.

The Talyllyn Railway was inspiration for the series of children's books, Thomas the Tank Engine.

Top tips

- Wear trail running shoes – it gets extremely muddy
- Take a gel or two if you're going to be out any longer than 1:45
- Make a weekend out of it – it's a shame to travel such a long way and not make more of the scenery. The after-party is great too!

28 COMRADES MARATHON

Durban/Pietermoritzburg, South Africa | ∿ Road | 1166m | 12 May | ⊕ www.comrades.com

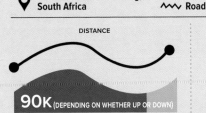

DISTANCE

90K (DEPENDING ON WHETHER UP OR DOWN)

HR	MIN	SEC
0 5	2 0	4 9

FASTEST TIME (DOWN)

0 5	2 4	0 0

FASTEST TIME (UP)

0 8	2 3	4 4

TOBIAS' FINISHING TIME

76% COMPLETION RATE

One question I'm often asked is, 'What's the best race I've ever done?' But as this book illustrates, picking just one race to do before you die is pretty hard work. Each and every race here has got something to offer. But Comrades Marathon is something truly special. Not only is it the world's largest ultra-marathon, it's also the oldest one still going today – which means it has bucket-loads of character.

First run in 1921, it was the inspiration of World War I veteran Vic Clapham, who having survived a 2,700km march through East Germany during the war, returned home to South Africa determined to commemorate 'Man's spirit over adversity'. Inspired by the Stock Exchange London to Brighton Walk, he wanted to create a similar event, starting in his hometown of Pietermaritzburg and finishing up in the coastal town of Durban. As both the South African athletics body and the League of Comrades of the Great War, after which the race was named, thought the 90km distance 'far too strenuous for even a trained athlete', the race almost didn't happen.

Thank goodness it did because the Comrades Marathon is, in my humble opinion, one of the greatest races on the planet. It's a race that has over the past 90 years brought a troubled country together, united under a common goal: to get to the finish. Old grievances are put aside, as men and women of every creed, colour and background attempt to make it to the finish before the brutal 12-hour cut-off. It's the manner in which the cut-off is put into effect that's the most controversial. A man stands with his back to the oncoming runners and at the exact second of the hour, fires a pistol in the air, at which point anyone behind him is prevented from continuing, even if they are just one second over the cut-off. These points are scattered along the course but missing the one at the end is the most disappointing of all.

In order to get a slot, you need to complete an officially recognised race (marathon

It's still dark when the race begins at 5 a.m., signalled by a cock crowing.

distance and beyond, including Ironman) in the preceding year. The time in which you complete it determines your all-important starting pen. And because this is a gun-to-gun event, if you're at the back, then that 10-plus minutes of waiting time eats into your already precious cut-off time.

The start of the race is one of the most atmospheric I've ever witnessed. From the national anthem to the singing of the 'Miners' Song', a real tear-jerker, you're swept up in the emotion of this race. It's not for nothing that it's called the Ultimate Human Race. You'll want to learn the lyrics simply so you can join in. And once the cock crows (which is the recording of a man's voice), that's your cue:

because you now have 12 hours to get to the finish, wherever that may be.

Now if you're thinking it's easy to run 89km in 12 hours, you might be right. In comparison to many other ultra-marathons, 89km isn't a particularly long way. But most marathons don't have to contend with the 'Big Five' hills and dozens of smaller ones in between. Indeed, this race is the definition of 'undulating'. It doesn't even matter in which direction you choose to do the race. If it starts at Pietermaritzburg and finishes in Durban, then it's called a 'Down' run; if it starts in Durban, then it's an 'Up' run. Both have their challenges.

I'd high hopes of getting the coveted silver medal – awarded to those who run between

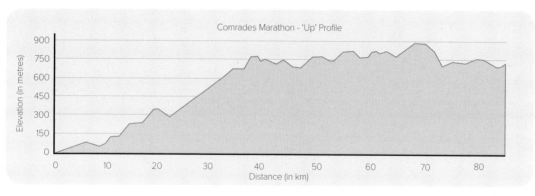

Comrades Marathon - 'Up' Profile

6 and 7:30. And with a marathon PB of 2:49, it was not beyond my abilities. So I latched myself onto those with Green Numbers (a permanent race number awarded to those who've completed more than 10 Comrades Marathons) in the hope that their experience would get me to the finish. But there were several things I hadn't quite factored in.

First, those hills – they suck the life out of your legs. If I'd thought it was bad going up, I never expected it to hurt so much going down. During the final 30km, I was reduced to a hobble. Second, trying to run a three-hour marathon pace on the road for 90km hurts – a lot! Third, you can never have enough gels. Normally I'm not a huge fan (they can upset the stomach) but you'll consume anything that will keep you going. Fourth, it may well be autumn in South Africa, but it's still extremely hot under the African sun. By the time I reached the finish, I was a perspiring wreck of a man.

But there was one other thing I wasn't prepared for, even though I'd read about it – namely, the overwhelming support from the roadside, where it feels as if the entire country has come out to cheer you on. From the early hours of the morning people will gather to set up their *braais* (barbecues) and with a beer in one hand and a piece of meat in the other, shout words of encouragement at you. Sadly, even the promise of cold lager or meat wasn't enough to coax my legs to go any faster and once I realised my dreams of a silver medal were over, I settled for a no less respectable Bill Rowan Medal (awarded to those who finish between 7:30 and 9 hours).

They say you've only truly run Comrades when you've done it in both directions – for which, if you do your first two back to back, you earn a special medal. And if you've got real grit and stamina, you could be like Dave Rogers from Hillcrest, South Africa, who has completed it a record-breaking 45 times (his first Comrades was in 1961 when he was just 18). But even if you get to do it just once, that's enough to see why this is the Ultimate Human Race.

Top tips

- Wear the most comfortable trainers you have in your possession
- Be careful who you accept water sachets from – dirty hands can quickly turn to diarrhoea and vomiting
- Take a sun cap but be aware it has to have no logo (except for the main sponsor)

The route follows many of the main roads between Durban and Pietermaritzburg.

29

ORIGINAL MOUNTAIN MARATHON

UK, Location changes each year

Fell and mountain

4,000m+ for Elite to 2,000m for D Class

October

www.omm.com

DISTANCE

FROM **40–80K**

HR MIN SEC

0 9 1 3 4 6

TIMES DEPENDENT ON RACE CLASS

1 3 1 0 4 2

TOBIAS' FINISHING TIME

70% COMPLETION RATE

Defeat came three hours into Day 1 of a 50km race into the Cumbrian hills surrounding Ullswater. 'Sorry, mate, I'm not going to make it,' I told my race partner as another spasm of cramp coursed through my quads, the contours of my grimace as wild as those of the mountain that beat me. I had underestimated the Original Mountain Marathon (OMM), a two-day race-cum-orienteering event that tests your mountain skills as well as your leg muscles. But that was in 2005, back in the day when it was called the Karrimor International Mountain Marathon (KIMM). After a change of sponsor and a new name, I returned four years later – and this time I was determined to complete it.

Always held on the last weekend of October, the OMM has been running since 1968. Three thousand hardy souls travel to a location in the UK that changes every year but is always remote and always what fell runners from the

At night, the sea of over a thousand tents is a sight worth seeing.

North might describe as 'undulating'. Like other mountain events, you work in a team (of two in this case), carrying everything you need on your back: a sleeping bag, tent and enough food for the 36 hours. GPS devices are not allowed so you must arm yourself with a map and compass to navigate your way over boggy ground, up and down hernia-inducing hills, across rocky mountain streams and heather-strewn valleys. All the while looking for checkpoints usually located in the middle of a bog.

The OMM has eight different courses to enter depending on your experience. They range from an 80km elite race to a 40km option for keen novices and half-day checkpoint events for those with hill-walking experience. The key to completing the 65km A class that we'd entered is specific training and finding the sweet spot between packing enough food and warm clothing – and therefore staying as light as possible. Although the elite runners can fit everything they need into a 10–15-litre rucksack, don't make any compromises that could leave you cold or hungry overnight. Believe me, morale is dependent on food. The perceived wisdom is that you need 4,000kcal to

Maps are only handed out at the start – so the ability to navigate on the fly is key.

ensure you have the energy for the second day's run. Compact, high-calorie foods such as cold pizza or condensed fruit bars are ideal. And for Day 1, you also can risk taking something more substantial to eat within the first couple of hours, like a sandwich or a bagel. After all, you won't be carrying this weight for long.

Choosing a good partner is also crucial. Although I was a quicker runner than my partner in my second OMM, he was more experienced in the hills and a better navigator – a handy combination when faced with 12+ hours of running through bog, fell, marsh and heather. You should also bear in mind the winners of the Elite category run at a seven-hour marathon pace, so speed is not an issue. The key is to focus your training on getting used to running (particularly descending) on uneven ground and, of course, practise your navigation skills too. It doesn't matter how fast you're going if you're running in the wrong direction!

Building on these foundations, and the fact that my partner was a very strong navigator, we thoroughly enjoyed ourselves, completing the course in a total time of 13 hours and 10 minutes. It was without doubt one of the most enjoyable weekends I've spent in the hills. And although we were cold, wet and occasionally lost, I finally put the OMM demon to rest and conquered the mountain.

BELOW: Always held on the last weekend of October, the weather for this run is often fickle.

RIGHT: The location, which is kept secret until several months before the race, changes each year.

Top tips

- Less is more: the lighter your kit, the faster you'll run

- If you're uncertain of your navigation ability, enter one of the shorter courses. The Elite Long Score is for those with previous OMMs under their belt

- If you can't find a suitable teammate, ask the organisers. There are others in the same position

30

BRAEMAR GATHERING HILL RACE

📍 Braemar, Scotland 〰 Fell 🏛 390m 📅 September 🌐 www.braemargathering.org

DISTANCE

3.5 Miles

HR MIN SEC
00 24 28
FASTEST TIME (KNOWN)

00 40 30
TOBIAS' FINISHING TIME

99% COMPLETION RATE

It would be true to say that I've become something of an aficionado of hill racing and fell running almost by accident. Sometimes your first experience of something leaves an indelible mark, either for good or ill. Certainly my very first attempt to run up a rough, heather-covered and rocky mountainous slope was not entirely by choice.

In my army days, in 2006 my regiment was attending the Braemar Royal Highland Gathering, an event known throughout the world, not least because of the high-profile attendees – none other than Her Majesty The Queen and other members of the Royal Family. The Queen is known for her support of the Armed Forces and my colonel thought it would be only appropriate if a few of the junior officers took part. It was already clear that none of us were up to tossing the caber, this being a specialist activity not readily embraced by us 'flatlanders'. However, we could all run.

So, what better idea than to propose that we should take part in the famous Morrone Hill Race? This being not so much a suggestion as an order, I braced myself for what was to follow: the run, apparently, was around 3.5 miles with just 1,300 feet of ascent.

The Morrone, whose name also translates as 'Big Hill' or 'Big Nose' has been raced up and down ever since 1832, having moved hills from the slightly smaller, but neighbouring Creag Choinnich, which had been first raced up in around 1068, giving it the distinction of being if not the world's oldest hill race, certainly the most ancient in Great Britain. The race starts with a 400m lap of the grass athletics track, amidst cheers, applause and the whirl and skirl of the bagpipes and general revelry. It's easy to forget that this is simply designed to spread out the field a little and dull your senses somewhat to what lies ahead.

Once you exit from the arena you are, so to speak, let loose rather like hounds off a lead! We were told firmly of the cut-off of 45 minutes and if we failed to meet it, there would be no chance of returning through the gate we had just passed: it would be shut firmly in our faces. Furthermore, to add to the ignominy of being tardy, we would not be allowed back into the arena. I had no intention of suffering such a fate, and set off at a cracking pace, with my usual enthusiasm, trusting my legs would speed me to the top without any difficulty. However, I hadn't bargained on quite so many rocks and zig-zags, to say nothing of a degree of uncertainty about which way really was the fastest to the top. Puffing more than I had supposed, I reached the five-cairns sitting atop the hill and was able to draw breath for a few seconds to gaze out at the stunning panoramic view across the Cairngorms. And of course to receive the wristband given to every runner who makes it to this, the highest point.

The Braemar Royal Highland Gathering.

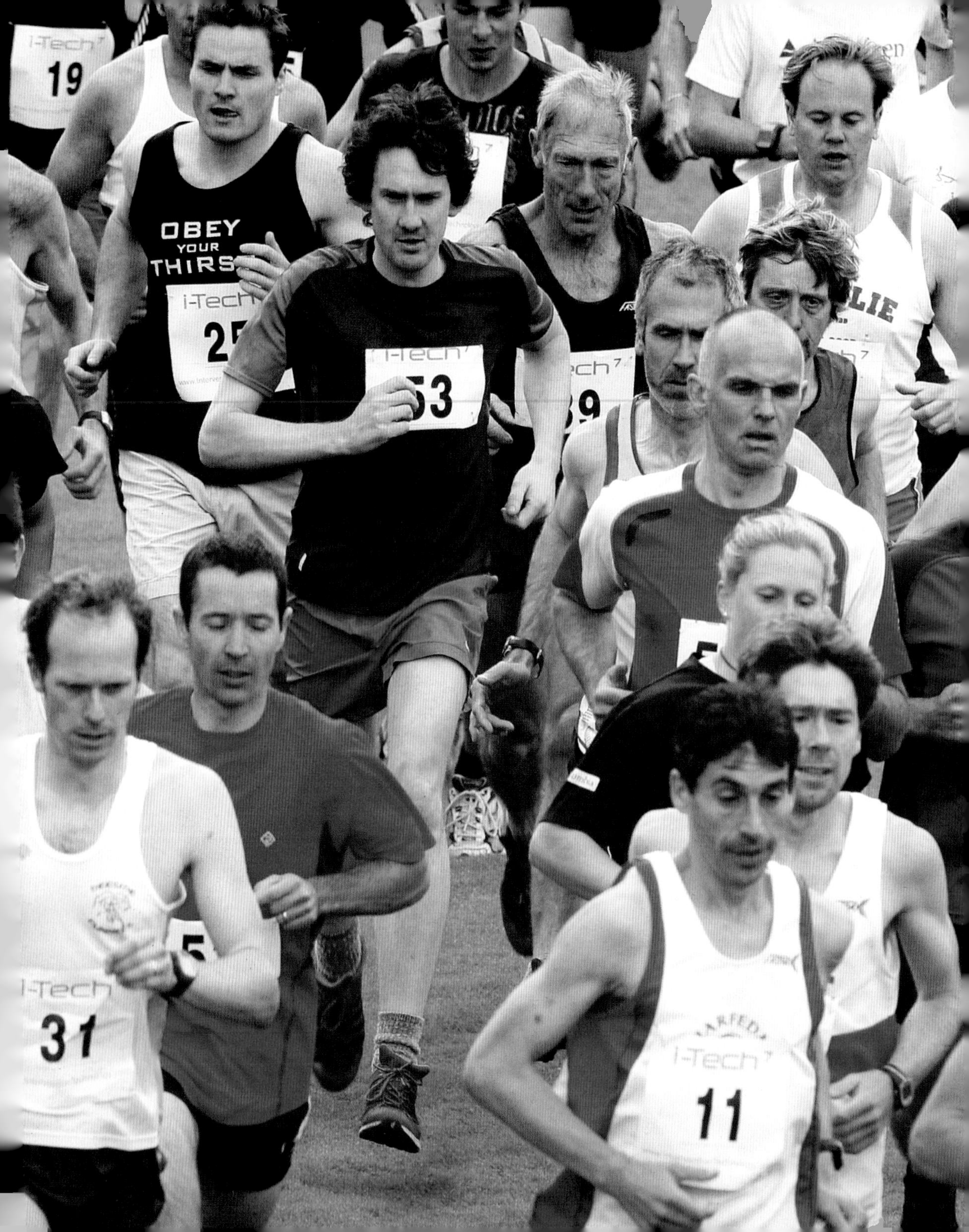

i-Tech
19
OBEY
YOUR
53
31
11

But there was no time to lose and it was here that I first realised it might be one thing to get to the top but quite another to get down. The route to the bottom was far harder than the route up, and there was absolutely no way to see which would be the fastest one to take. Not to say the smoothest, although there was little chance of that. However, I was not prepared to follow the example of some of my fellow contestants and apply my seat to the ground, but keeping my feet on it proved a considerable challenge.

What I thought would be a bit of a breeze turned out to be a surprise. I did make it through the gate on both legs, though I will admit they were scratched, sore and not in the best of shape for the triumphant final lap around the arena, where I finished in 40:30 – a full 15 minutes behind the winner. However, the cheers and clapping of the crowd were amazing. And as at that time a serving officer, the presence of the Head of the Armed Forces applauding lent a certain atmosphere not to be found in every fell race.

I can only say that it was a grand experience and one that did in fact give me a taste for future adventures on hills and fells. If you should find yourself in the vicinity of Braemar on the first Saturday of September, I can heartily recommend you give it a go.

The start of the race begins with a lap of the grass athletics track, under the watchful eye of the HM The Queen.

Top tips

- It's easier to follow the trail up then down, where anything goes
- Place your hands on your knees to help alleviate back pain

31 RED BULL STEEPLECHASE

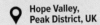 Hope Valley, Peak District, UK

 Fell

 1,400m

 October

 steeplechase.redbull.co.uk

DISTANCE

21 Miles (FULL COURSE)

HR	MIN	SEC
0 2	3 5	0 0

FASTEST TIME (KNOWN) FULL COURSE

0 3	1 9	2 8

TOBIAS' FINISHING TIME (27TH)

8% COMPLETION RATE

With any race, there's always a chance you'll not finish. But it's rare that you enter a race where you're almost *guaranteed* not to finish. Ironically, this is the whole point of the Red Bull Steeplechase. Set in the Peak District, this is a fell race with a cruel twist: only the top 30 men and 10 women out of the 500 entrants is allowed to finish, the remainder being knocked out at the various steeples enroute. Those who finish the full course will have run 21 miles and climbed 1,400m. Of course, being sponsored by Red Bull, a company with a reputation for lending their name to quirky, yet tough events, it therefore attracts a wide range of athletes, from ultra-runners and adventure racers to local fell runners and marathoners.

The race starts a few miles away from the finish at Castleton. In true Red Bull fashion, and ensuring that everyone gets their fair taste of grit in the first section, it begins with a brutal climb up the side of Mam Tor. With no set route, it was a case of finding our own way to the top, using grass, plant routes and anything else we could find to drag ourselves up the near-vertical hill. But once on the top, we were rewarded

with a stunning run along the Barker Bank ridge line, offering panoramic views of the Lake District. I would have loved to stop to admire the view, but a previous competitor had advised that I needed to be in 35th position by the first steeple at Bamford if I was to stand a chance of completing all four legs and making it to the finish. As far as I was concerned, not finishing wasn't an option!

By the time I'd reached Bamford in 40th position, having run eight miles and gained 580m in elevation, I could understand how many of the runners (165, to be precise) would be delighted to go no further. But like a game where your success elongates the agony, I continued, determined to see it through to the bitter end.

Section 2 was shorter – a mere four miles, but had 310m of elevation – so basically it felt as

Although the Peak District's hills might not be as high as those found in the neighbouring Lakes, they're just as severe.

Top tips:

- Take decent fell shoes with lots of grip

- If you want to finish the full course, then you'll need to be in the top 35 going through the first steeple

OPPOSITE: Only 40 out of 500 starters will make it to the finish.

RIGHT: With over 1,400m of ascent compounded within 21 miles, it's likely you'll look a little worse for wear.

if I was running uphill for most of it. I'd glance at the runners alongside me, trying to judge whether or not they were faster than me. But I've learned never to judge a book by its cover and in this field of fell runners, obstacle course races, ultra-runners and the odd elite marathoner, anything was possible.

The terrain, some of which was on private land, was a blend of fell, trail and road. One moment we'd be flat out on a farm track and the next, tip-toeing between rocks, praying we didn't trip and fall – which of course some did. And although there were many talented runners, a number of them weren't having a good day. Knowing they wouldn't be able to go the full distance, they would pull up shy of the checkpoint to allow through those who did want to continue. For those of us who did, it was a true race – not just against the terrain, but every runner around you. With another third of the competitors knocked out of the race at Hope, it left a very nervous 125 men and 45 women to battle it out to the third and final steeple.

The six-mile Section 3, from Hope to Edale, was one of the most nerve-wracking experiences of my racing career. My legs were on the verge of cramp, my calves killing me from spending so much time on my toes, and I was desperately thirsty, not having drunk enough at the previous aid station. However, having gone through the second steeple in 32nd position, there was no time to lose and so I bounded along the single track, looking over my shoulder every so often like a hunted man.

Two hours and 40 minutes after I set off, I arrived at the third and final steeple, well and truly knackered. I almost thought I'd not made the cut-off, misreading one of the counters, but then realised I was in 26th position: I'd made it! In fact, it didn't matter how long it took me to finish the fourth and final section – unless I became lost or broke a leg – I could rightfully claim to be a full-course finisher. So I took my foot off the gas and enjoyed the last three miles back to Castleton, feeling exceptionally pleased with myself.

With the race complete, and a free hog roast on offer, it was time to eat, be merry and enjoy the remainder of an awesome day's running.

32 ENDURANCELIFE COASTAL TRAIL SERIES

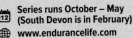

Series runs October – May (South Devon is in February)

📍 **Beesands, South Devon and across the UK**

〰️ **Trail and hills**

1,500m

🌐 **www.endurancelife.com**

DISTANCE

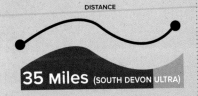

35 Miles (SOUTH DEVON ULTRA)

HR	MIN	SEC
0 4	4 3	0 0

FASTEST TIME (KNOWN)

| 0 5 | 1 3 | 0 0 |

TOBIAS' FINISHING TIME

71% COMPLETION RATE ULTRA

If you've ever harboured a desire to explore more of Britain's stunning coastline, simply enter one of the Endurancelife Coastal Trail Series events. Running from October until May, the series showcases the most iconic points on the British coastline, from South Devon to Dover and all the way up to Northumberland. At every location, there are four distances to choose from, a cheeky 10K, half marathon, marathon and even a punishing ultra – all depending upon your fitness levels and ability to withstand pain. But one thing is certain: whichever distance you choose, it's guaranteed to be beautiful and hilly.

Now in its eleventh year, the Coastal Trail Series has become one of the most popular series of trail races in the UK, something I can attest to, having done three of their events, including the grand-daddy of them all, the South Devon Ultra. With South Devon being the birthplace of the Coastal Trail Series, if you had to do just one, this 'cult classic' would be it!

The race starts in the charming fishing village of Beesands, not far from Kingsbridge. An Area of Outstanding Natural Beauty, it's a feast for the eyes and a beast on the legs. Jagged rocks, sandy coves, epic climbs and fantastic single tracks … it has all the ingredients for a memorable day out.

The atmosphere at these events is fantastic, helped by the fact that they begin on a Saturday morning, giving the perfect excuse to make a weekend of it. After all, it would be a shame to come all the way down to the South West of England and not take advantage of the infamous Devon hills, quaint villages and sandy coves, just perfect for picnics.

As the name suggests, the Coastal Trail Series takes you along some of Britain's most spectacular coastline.

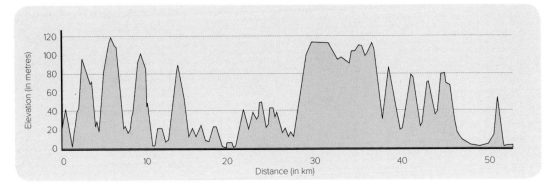

No matter what distance you choose, the first three miles of short and sharp climbs along the coastline result in a decent amount of huffing and puffing, especially approaching Start Point. But on reaching the Great Sleaden Rock, the course splits and those doing the 10K return back towards the start, whilst everyone else continues along the coast.

The organisers, Endurancelife, are acutely aware of the dangers of running along the British coastline and insist you carry a number of mandatory items, from a waterproof jacket and first aid kit through to sufficient water and a mobile phone – items that were reassuring to have on sections of the route.

The ultra-course follows at least 10 miles of coastline before turning at Biddlehead Point, just beyond Portsmouth Down and coming back on itself, retracing some parts of the route before turning inland just before East Prawle, at around the 15-mile point. Here, the terrain changes from beautiful single track to the bridleways and footpaths of the Devon Hills, but it is no less challenging. The hills hurt just as much, the ground is boggy in places and, thanks to the high hedges, one is denied any form of view.

And then you reach the sting in the tail, when having already run the best part of the 28 miles, you pass the finish area of the marathon, only to continue and repeat the 10K loop down to Start Point and back. Mentally, the ultra is tough; physically, it's exhausting. Not only are you asking your legs to keep moving for another seven miles, you're politely asking the 10K runners, who have started three hours after the ultra, if they will let you pass.

But the best bit of all is that when it's all over, there's the option of taking a cold, yet refreshing dip in the sea, happy in the knowledge that you've run an ultra-marathon before lunch.

The CTS is so addictive, many runners try and complete the entire series.

Top tips

- As the South Devon Ultra race takes place in February, a windcheater or arm warmers will prove invaluable
- With the ground being slippery in places, you'll need a trail shoe with plenty of grip
- Leave your iPod and headphones at home and enjoy the sound of the waves crashing upon the rocks.

33 WINDERMERE MARATHON

📍 **Lake Windermere, Lake District, UK** 〰 **Road**  **500m+** 📅 **May** 🌐 **windermeremarathon.com**

DISTANCE

26.2 Miles

HR	MIN	SEC
0 2	2 3	1 6

FASTEST TIME (KNOWN)

| 0 3 | 0 7 | 2 5 |

TOBIAS' FINISHING TIME

CUT-OFF: 6.30

98% COMPLETION RATE

If anyone tells you that the Windermere Marathon is flat, they'd be lying to you! 'Lumpy and rolling' would do a better job of describing this surprisingly tough yet scenic marathon that does a complete circuit of England's largest lake. But take into account this is the tenth and final marathon in the Brathay 10in10 and you'll quit complaining and marvel at those who bravely run this course every day for 10 days – all in aid of the Brathay Hall Trust.

Fingers on stopwatches, runners patiently wait for the signal to start.

The Windermere Marathon has been running since 1982 and has held various accolades, including being crowned the UK's most 'scenic marathon' by *Runner's World* magazine. But it wasn't until 2007, at the 60th anniversary of the Brathay Trust, a charity established to help vulnerable children and young people, that the 10in10 first took place.

The race, which starts and finishes in the splendid grounds of Brathay Hall, takes runners in an anti-clockwise direction around Lake Windermere. But this is a race where good manners are on display: an hour before the main event begins everyone walks down Brathay Hall's long driveway to see off the intrepid 10in10ers. By this stage, many of them are held together by a combination of Rocktape and pure grit, all determined to finish. This was to be their final marathon and quite possibly, the most emotional of the week. As I watched them move off, their movements almost robotic, I couldn't help but feel huge admiration for their exceptional efforts.

It was now our turn to run. With Lake Windermere glistening in the sun before us,

Drummers lead a procession of runners to the start.

we assembled on the front lawn of Brathay Hall before being led out by a local drumming band towards the start line. The atmosphere was electric as a large number of the runners were friends or family of the 10in10ers. This was their way of saying, 'We salute you!' Having not run nine marathons previously, we were a lot less robotic in our movements. But with the first three miles of the race being a gradual climb, it took many of us more than a few minutes to find our stride.

I've already mentioned the hills, but I'll do so again here. Although not of Alpine standards, the undulations are relentless, giving you the feeling of being on a roller coaster. And then occasionally, there's the odd climb that will bring all but the strongest runners to a staggering gait, particularly the mile-long effort, around seven miles in.

You don't get an especially clear view of Lake Windermere in the first half as your mind is occupied with trying to maintain some form of pace. It's not until you reach Newby Bridge at the bottom of the lake that the landscape opens up and a good view is afforded of not just the lake but the surrounding hills too. More importantly, it feels like the symbolic halfway point – although around a mile shy.

Being a charity-run event, the support on the course is first class. Every single one of the marshals, all of whom are volunteers, goes out of their way to ensure you have what you need at the aid stations. Add to the fact that each of the villages you pass through, from

Hawkshead through to Ambleside, makes you feel welcome, cheering you on as you pass.

By the time I reached top of the lake, and therefore was not far from Brathay Hall, I was almost sad to be finishing. The spirit of the event, the atmosphere, the people, the stunning scenery, the fact that you get to run around England's largest lake … it's easy to see why people keep coming back for more. And seeing the finishers of the 10in10, I marvelled at how running can bring so much pain, yet so much happiness!

Top tips

- Incorporate some hill training into your program – you'll need it!
- Learn who the 10in10ers are for the year you do it. That way you can appreciate what they've gone through to get there
- Make a weekend out of it – there's so much to see and do around Windermere

BELOW LEFT: Many races feel like a community, and Windermere Marathon is one of the friendliest events of its kind.

BELOW: Formed 13,000 years ago, Windermere is the largest natural lake in England.

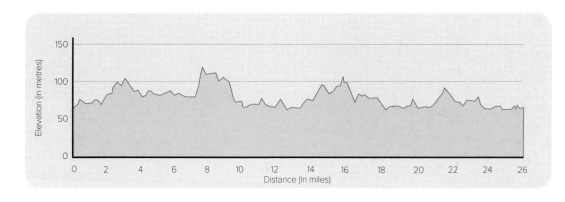

SUCKER FOR PUNISHMENT

34 GRIZZLY

 Devon, UK   Mud, trail, beach, bog, hilly   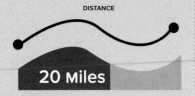 3,500ft

 March

 axevalleyrunners.org.uk/grizzly

DISTANCE

20 Miles

HR   MIN   SEC
0 2 1 1 0 0
FASTEST TIME (KNOWN)

0 2 4 3 2 3
TOBIAS' FINISHING TIME

99%
COMPLETION RATE

Ask any runner from the South West of England about the Grizzly and you'll be met with a series of grins, grimaces and other facial contortions interspersed with deep exhalations of breath as they try to describe what's involved in completing one of the UK's most popular and arguably toughest trail races. Even the race organisers, the Axe Valley Runners, struggle with a valid description, merely describing the race on their website as

OPPOSITE: The race begins on the Seaton esplanade.

ABOVE: The sound of 2,000 pairs of feet running on a shingle beach is impressive.

'Twentyish muddy, hilly, boggy, beachy miles of the multiest-terrain running experience you will find this side of the end of time.' From my experience of doing the race, this is just the tip of the iceberg.

Starting and finishing in the seaside town of Seaton, on East Devon's Jurassic Coast, it's a veritable get-together of running clubs, proven by the technicolour rainbow of club vests on the start line, alongside a decent number of yellow ones from the aforementioned Axe Valley Runners. Every year, since it was founded in 1988, the Grizzly adopts a different motto. In 2012, the year I did it, it was 'Every Hill has a Silver Lining'. In 2015 it was 'Dash to Delirium', but I think my favourite, and perhaps the most fitting of all, is the 2004 motto of 'Insanity and in Health'.

Whether you run near the water's edge
or higher up – it's still hard work.

There are two beach sections that will have you desperate for dry land.

Top tips:

- Wear your smile – especially on the hills, the beach and the bogs
- Take it easy on the beach section – it's harder than it looks
- Tie your laces tightly in case you lose a shoe in the Bog!

The Grizzly is the sort of race which unless you've done it, you might not have heard of. Which is an oxymoron in itself. And that might be because the Grizzly is a bit of a guarded secret. Indeed, 2016 will mark the 28th edition of this race. A race that despite the tough nature of the course has become so popular, they've had to introduce a ballot to pick out the 'lucky' 2,500 runners who will get a place.

Arriving in Seaton you'll notice immediately this race simply oozes character. When the Seaton town crier reads out a poem at the start, there's a hint of what's in store for you. And then, with the flourish of his bell, you're off!

Having foolishly placed myself at the front of the race, I was initially leading the way, without

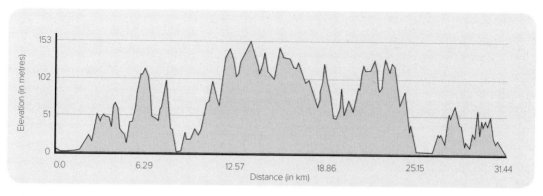

a clue where I was going, or what was coming up next. But as soon as my feet touched the half-mile of shingle beach, I could understand why this race is so revered. The sound of several thousand pairs of feet chewing through the pebbles makes an incredible noise, so when I finally found myself back on hard ground, this was not only a relief to my legs but also to my senses. But my joy of being off the beach was short-lived as we slogged up the first of what seemed like a thousand hills.

If ever a course was designed to disorientate you, this is it. Thank goodness it's marked. There are more twists and turns than a plate of noodles. And with every turn came a little surprise. A Scottish piper, a man playing the didgeridoo, the scent of incense on the Himalayan shrine complete with prayer flags … your imagination will run wild. One of the things I loved most about the race was the motivational signs helpfully placed along the route. My favourite was '7/5ths of the UK population don't understand fractions', which actually made me guffaw out loud. One of the many cheery support marshals en route, almost all of whom appeared to have sweets to hand out, saw me laughing and teasingly denied me a jelly baby, saying I looked to be enjoying myself too much. I reassured him I wasn't, before snatching a sweet from his outstretched hand

like a hungry animal and wearily making my way up another crippling hill.

As I continued along the route, I was acutely aware that the main highlight, the infamous Bog, was still to come. Even on a dry day, it's a quagmire of gigantic proportions and graveyard to many a missing trainer. I was silently relieved I wasn't going through it alone because if I got stuck, I'd need help to get out. Like a snail leaving a trail of mud and water, I shuffled my way along the twisting paths, watching the miles count down (they do mile markers in reverse to mess with your head) before hitting the 'Stairway to Heaven', which appeared to have more steps than the Empire State Building. Steps carved into the edge of a cliff, it was the final nail in the coffin.

With currents of cramp coursing through my body, I eventually reached the top to be rewarded with a view of the finish – exactly where I'd started, about two and a half hours earlier. With renewed energy, I merrily bounced down the hill, quads wincing with pain, before running the final stretch along the promenade and crossing the line in 15th place.

Whilst being hosed down by the local fire brigade, I felt as if I'd just unlocked the keys to a magical portal – one of pain but also memories that have stayed with me ever since. Mark my words, this is one of the best races you'll ever do!

HARD AS NAILS

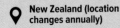

HARD AS NAILS

GODZONE ADVENTURE RACE

New Zealand (location changes annually)

Trail, river, road, mountain

 February

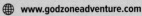 www.godzoneadventure.com

DISTANCE

530KM

HR   MIN   SEC

8 9 3 6 0 0

FASTEST TIME (KNOWN)

1 4 0 2 2 0 0

TOBIAS' FINISHING TIME

50% COMPLETION RATE FULL COURSE

'I'm not sure I can go on,' I say to my two teammates, as I peel off my socks to reveal the soles of my white feet, which thanks to being wet for the past several days have large, deep-set wrinkles. They are also incredibly sore.

For the past 48 hours I'd been clinging on for survival, using every ounce of my mental strength to keep me going – at least until the transition. Having foolishly not changed my socks after sea kayaking around Kaikoura Bay and mountain biking through the dense foliage of the Puhi Peaks, the 35-hour trek up a 2,885m peak that followed was the final straw for my poor feet. Every step felt as if I was walking on hot ambers of coal. With only a few hours' sleep, I hadn't had enough time to dry my feet out. And with at least another three days to go, for the first time in my life I wanted to quit.

Now, strictly speaking the GODZone isn't really a running race. It's an adventure race, but I'm including it because it's really, really good! For the uninitiated, the GODZone is a non-stop

530km expedition-style adventure race in New Zealand. Every year the location of the race changes, but you're guaranteed the adventure of a lifetime. But that of course depends upon whether you like the idea of trekking across wild terrain, climbing mountains, canoeing down rivers, sea kayaking amongst dolphins and mountain biking across private land, all with virtually no sleep.

For me, the GODZone was a race of firsts: my first adventure race, my first-time sea kayaking, my first Grade 3 rapids, my first time in New Zealand and perhaps most importantly, the first time I'd met my teammates, who all hailed from various parts of the world. Unlike marathon running or triathlons, it's fair to say adventure racing isn't a mainstream sport; it's hard, expensive and you need to have a wide skill set. That said, it's an enormous challenge that has its own rewards.

If you're wondering whether you could indeed 'do it', imagine running the Ultra-Trail

du Mont-Blanc, immediately followed by an Ironman, then the Devizes to Westminster Canoe Race and finishing off with La Ruta de los Conquistadores mountain bike race. Doing all of that with barely any sleep and navigating with a map and compass might give you a better idea of the GODZone.

What sets expedition-length adventure races like the GODZone apart from your standard endurance race is that they're non-stop. And by that I mean the clock starts on a Saturday and only stops when you cross the finish line, sometimes as long as 10 days later. You're self-supported, carrying everything you need to survive for the stage, swapping equipment and picking up food as you reach transition areas.

Teams make their way through the Inland Kaikoura Range of New Zealand's Southern Alps.

It's also a team event that must include at least one person from the opposite sex. You must also stay within 100m of each other, so trying to find a team that has the requisite skills and with whom you're compatible is no small feat. Moreover, if one of you fails to complete the course, you become 'unranked'. Sadly, we lost our female companion after Stage 3. The route is kept secret until the day of the race, when you're given a few hours to work out where you need to go and what food and equipment you'll need for each stage. The next chance to rest will be in about a week's time.

ABOVE: With the majestic Southern Alps as their backdrop, there's plenty of time to reflect.

OPPOSITE TOP: Although taking place in summer, it isn't uncommon to see snow high up in the mountains.

OPPOSITE BOTTOM: You'll have the chance to negotiate some Grade 3 rapids of the Clarence River.

Forty-eight hours into the race, and I'm sitting down eating some food whilst trying to air my feet. My mind had already quit, but if I did, so must my team. Knowing that they relied on me to continue was a heavy burden, but mine to bear. A few hours' rest allowed my head to calm and my body to recover. Today was not the day to quit.

Luckily, the next stage was a night-time 100-mile mountain bike ride through the Molesworth estate through to Hanmer Springs. When not fighting off the sleep monsters, the ride was a welcome reprieve from being on my feet. But it was short-lived, as the subsequent 24-hour long mountain trek was the stuff of nightmares for someone suffering immersion foot. A bad route choice resulted in us following a stream from source to river, walking down its slippery riverbed through the night for more than 13 hours. I shudder just thinking about it.

As the lack of sleep takes its toll, irritability levels rise and your sense of humour starts to wane. But then this is where the banter of your team holds you together; the common goal of getting to the end and knowing that you need each other.

After the initial 48 hours, which felt as if they'd lasted forever, the subsequent three days passed relatively quickly. A 100km canoe down the Hurunui River, a short two-hour mountain bike stage, a tough orienteering-style coastal

trek, another mountain bike stage and we're on the final stretch – a 30km sea kayak stage back to Kaikoura in the company of a pod of dolphins.

When people ask me what's the toughest race I've ever done, the GODZone features pretty high on the list. It was not just a journey through the heart of the South Island of New Zealand, but through my mind, stretching the boundaries of my self-imposed limitations to the point where I came out the other end a virtually new man. Sadly, the same didn't apply for my feet!

Top tips

- Ensure you have at least a 2-Star Kayak/canoe competency course under your belt
- Choose the most comfortable trail shoes you can find. You'll be spending an enormous amount of time on your feet
- Ensure at least two of you in the team can navigate

ABOVE: While wading across estuaries, efforts to keep your clothes dry will often be in vain.

LEFT: The final stage involves a 25km sea kayak back to the Kaikoura Peninsula, with dolphins swimming in the background.

 TRANSALPINE-RUN

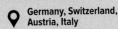 Germany, Switzerland, Austria, Italy

Mountain trails, technical

16,310m

 September

 en.transalpine-run.com

DISTANCE

268K
(2010 EDITION WAS 320KM)

HR	MIN	SEC
3 4	0 6	5 3

FASTEST INDIVIDUAL TIME (KNOWN)
(FASTEST TEAM: SALOMON IN 28:29:27)

4 2	1 2	2 4

TOBIAS' FINISHING TIME 15TH/75

60%
COMPLETION RATE

When I tell people about the Gore-Tex Transalpine-Run, I often think to myself how barmy it sounds: 300km in eight days of running across four countries (Switzerland, Italy, Germany and Austria), with a mind-boggling 16,000m of ascent on out-of-this-earth trails in one the most stunning mountain ranges in the world. What's not to like about that? And although your nearest and dearest might be slightly alarmed by these figures, to an ultra-runner, it's music to his ears.

Now in its eleventh year, the Transalpine-Run was first held in 2005 and has developed a bit of a cult reputation in the trail-running world, with the result that all of its 300 team entries are filled months before race day. Being a team race, you need to consider rather carefully whose company you wish to keep for eight long days, running together up to 300km. It's a very small list. I chose an army friend who'd run the Jungle Marathon several years earlier and I felt sure would be up to the challenge.

Unlike many other multi-stage ultra-marathons, which require you to carry all your essential equipment and belongings, the only things you need with you are emergency items of kit, such as a waterproof jacket, warm top, gloves, hat and a mobile phone. All of these you might be glad of, when ascending 3,000m-high mountains.

LEFT: The Tre Cime di Lavaredo provides a stunning backdrop.

OPPOSITE: Crystal blue lakes, waterfalls, forests, snow-capped mountains – the Transalpine-Run has it all.

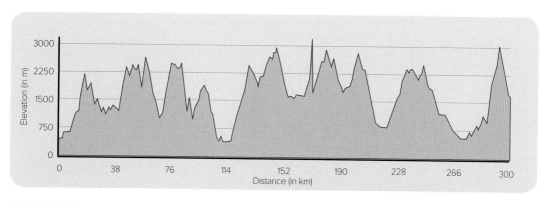

OPPOSITE: Emerging from the clouds at the summit of a peak, the view is to die for. If only there was time to look back and enjoy it!

ABOVE: Being a team event, runners must stay together in their pairs at all times.

In the precursor to the race, there's plenty to agonise over. Have I trained enough? What happens if either I or my teammate becomes injured? What running shoes should I use? What hydration pack should I go for? And the eternal question: to take running poles or not? I'd spent hours brooding over these questions, but as soon as my teammate and I stood on the start line, listening to AC/DC blasting out on the tannoy, the excitement of simply being there absorbed all of our senses. Suddenly, none of the things mattered as we entered an alpine bubble of eye-wateringly beautiful scenery that would take our breath away.

There is a choice of staying in hotels each night or a slightly cheaper and more authentic route of sleeping on the floor of sports centres, along with several hundred runners, many of whom aren't quite so bashful as the British when getting changed. The latter option is by far the best way to soak up the experience and to make friends, but it does mean that you'll occasionally wake up in the middle of the night to an international concerto of snores, coughs and, well, other noises.

Besides getting a good night's sleep, your main effort is ensuring that neither of you becomes injured. My teammate sadly had to withdraw after five days, having developed a nasty knee problem. The terrain is brutal and with so much climbing and descending, your knees and ankles won't be thanking you. And if one of you does drop out, then you'll not have an official team ranking, but be an 'Individual Finisher'.

When running through the Dolomites, one can't fail to be awestruck by their beauty.

To run across four countries is an extraordinary feeling, especially as you'll start in the German Alps and finish up in the Italian Alps or vice versa, as the route alternates in direction each year. Either way you get to run through parts of the mighty Dolomites otherwise not normally on the tourist trail. But what makes this event so great – and it is in my opinion, one of the greatest trail running events in the world – is the people you meet. Every night it's a party atmosphere, as you have a beer and relax after a long day's running.

And when you share your photos with your nearest and dearest, they will totally understand the allure of the Transalpine-Run.

Top tips

- Nordic walking poles could be a godsend
- Make sure you refuel sufficiently to hydrate and top up your carb stores each night
- Carry a small pack then you're less likely to take unnecessary stuff

37 JUNGLE ULTRA

Manu National Park, Peru | **Jungle trails and rivers** | **June** | www.beyondtheultimate.co.uk/jungleultra.asp

DISTANCE

230K (FIVE DAYS)

HR	MIN	SEC
18	11	00

FASTEST TIME (KNOWN)

| 28 | 22 | 00 |

TOBIAS' FINISHING TIME

73% COMPLETION RATE

Due to a modicum of genetic good fortune discovered late in life, the ability to run comes naturally to me. As you'll have discovered in the other sections of this book, I've successfully run multi-stage races in deserts and mountains, but as I plodded along a rocky track, 10,500ft high in the Andean Cloud Forest of Manu National Park in Peru, I could barely breathe, let alone put one foot in front of the other. It was as though someone had cruelly tied my laces together, sneakily stuffed my pack full of bricks and then, for good measure, put a plastic bag over my head. The truly depressing bit was that I'd not been 'running' for more than five minutes of the first stage of the inaugural Jungle Ultra and I still had 225km to go.

Multi-stage races are hard. The relentless assault on your body takes its toll. Carrying seven days' worth of food and equipment, you run for anything between four and fourteen hours, hope you arrive in one piece at the overnight camp, grab some food, tend to your feet, fall asleep and repeat the same every day for a week. There's no doubt about it, these types of races are brutal.

The start of the Jungle Ultra takes place over 10,000ft up in the Cloud Forest.

Part of a series of Ultimate Ultras (Jungle, Desert, Ice and Mountain), the Jungle Ultra is no different. A 230km, five-stage ultra-marathon that will have you running along virgin jungle trails, wading across streams and rivers, clambering up cliffs, zip-lining across gorges, crawling under and over fallen trees, trudging through mud, and plodding along at least 30 km of shingle riverbed. Somehow, all of this seemed like an attractive proposition to the other 17 international competitors lining up with me at the start of the race – despite constant humidity destroying not only our clothes, but also our bodies and the creatures waiting to feed off us.

With this being the first race of its kind in Peru, and the first by the race organisers Beyond the Ultimate, it was new to us all. When I asked how they decided upon the route, I was told that someone's uncle had once followed a path from such and such a route to the other side. But that was 40 years ago! So the paths we were following were literally virgin jungle trails. I felt like an intrepid explorer.

Unlike many other multi-stage events where tents are provided for you, one of the mandatory items on the kit list is a hammock. Now, I'm the first to admit that the idea of sleeping in a hammock sounds rather romantic but I can assure you, unless it's on a tropical beach, it's not. Many of us had never slept in one before let alone erected one, so there was the odd squeal as someone's hammock untied itself. Armed with just a silk liner we would lie awake, wrapping what clothing we could find around us, as none of us came adequately prepared for the severe drop in temperature during the night.

But as we made our way through the Amazon Basin, seeing giant fire ants, avoiding snakes, trudging through so many rivers I lost count, I couldn't help but respect the jungle and anyone who lives in it. Indeed, in the evenings we'd often camp with local tribes – who'd never seen anything like us before. And although we weren't supposed to accept, they kindly gave us samples of their food – crusty chicken thighs that looked dodgy but turned out to be delicious.

With almost every multi-stage race there is normally one day that's harder than all the others. And a casual observer would probably

Participants race along virgin jungle trails created for the race.

LEFT: With more than 75 river crossings, sometimes you need a helping hand.

BELOW: The villagers's enthusiastic cheers got Guy Jennings and I over the finish line.

think the 92km 'long stage' on Day 5 to be the one to fear. However, it's not. Stage 4 – named the Lull – is the true monster in this jungle adventure. It is the day that has no end, will see you climb hills so steep, you'll need the vines to pull you up, and coming down the other side requires the dexterity of a mountain goat.

Looking back on the moments when I was clinging to the root of a plant on the side of a vertical drop, fighting off ants, wading across rivers, staring at majestic waterfalls, laughing with newly made friends, meeting local tribes, accidentally blocking the only loo in the village and having to ask the village elder to unblock it – they're all memories I treasure to this day.

Top tips

- Practise sleeping in a hammock before the race
- Fingerless gloves are useful for preventing cuts to your hands
- Take sufficient warm kit for the evening – it can get cold

HARD AS NAILS

38 MARATHON DES SABLES

 Sahara Desert, Morocco   Desert, rocky ground, sand dunes   April 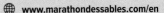 www.marathondessables.com/en

DISTANCE

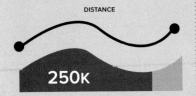

250K

	HR	MIN	SEC
	20	21	00

FASTEST TIME (KNOWN)

24 01 00

TOBIAS' FINISHING TIME

CUT-OFF: 10 HOURS (STAGES 1 AND 2); 10:30
(STAGE 3); 36 (STAGE 4); 12 (STAGE 5) = 78.5 HOURS
(APPROX. THE TIME OF THE SLOWEST PERSON)

90%
COMPLETION
RATE

You never need to worry about getting lost – just follow the person in front!

If ever there was one race that you need to consider, at some point in your life, then the Marathon des Sables (MdS) is probably it. Especially if you already call yourself an ultra-runner, because like it or not, that 'race in the desert' will be the first thing anyone asks if you've done. Also known as the Marathon of the Sands, it has captured the imagination of thousands of people through the course of its 30-year history.

Having twice completed this race, and therefore speaking from blister-induced experience, it's always easy to reflect upon how you'd do things differently if you had a second chance. Because generally speaking 'once in a lifetime races' aren't meant to happen, as the phrase hints, more than once – especially the MdS. Indeed, the pure expense of entering the race and investing enough time to train for it, let alone actually complete it, should be enough to put off a second attempt. But with 30 per cent of entrants being repeat offenders, it clearly has something to offer that entices people to come back for more, over and over again.

Held annually in April, the MdS is a 250km, six-day race across the Sahara Desert, in southern Morocco. And being self-supported, competitors have the added challenge of having to carry a daily minimum of 2,000 kcals of food with them as well as a sleeping bag and a few other compulsory items.

The first three stages – around 30–37km each day – are just the warm-up for the 'Long Day' on Stage 4, which is anywhere between 80 and 90km. It is the stage that every runner fears and which will either make or break you. The final stage is 'just' a marathon but is often underestimated in difficulty.

OPPOSITE: With AC/DC playing on loudspeakers, the start of each MDS stage is a memorable occasion.

Running on sand is not easy – but you get the hang of it after 250km.

Top tips

- The lighter your rucksack, the faster you'll run – try to get it to less than 7kg without water
- Learn to manage your feet – they will determine how much you enjoy the race
- Drink little and often. Dehydration is your enemy

The checkpoints provide a good opportunity to cool off.

That's simply because all the things that you do to keep yourself alive during the week, you disregard for the final day, thinking you 'have it in the bag'.

But no matter how much raw talent one may have, running around Clapham Common is not exactly the perfect training ground when preparing to race across sand dunes in the scorching heat of the Sahara Desert. Indeed, one afternoon in March, whilst trotting along Balham High Road, kitted out in what can only be described as 'full dress rehearsal', I was a cause of some puzzlement.

Some might say that anyone's enjoyment of the MdS is largely determined by two things: the number of blisters you acquire and how well you get along with your tent mates. You can avoid blisters by preparing your feet before hand with zinc oxide tape and simply identifying hotspots in advance. The same goes for your tent mates. Your choice of tent mates is up to you. You can choose them before the race, or as I did in 2013, as I arrived in the camp. But choose wisely – you'll spend a lot of time with them.

Unsurprisingly, it can get jolly hot in the desert. The average temperatures at the start of the race were mostly in the mid-thirties – very doable if acclimatised. But not even my hot Bikram yoga sessions could prepare me for the 54°C midday temperature that it rose to on Stage 4, the 75km Long Stage. And if you're at the business end of the field, pushing yourself to the edge of your endurance limits, even the elite athletes can succumb to the desert.

Now a member of the Ultra-Trail World Tour (UTWT) – a series of tough ultra-marathons from a body that promotes some of the most iconic trail races in the world – the MdS has started to attract a wide variety of elite athletes, all vying for a Top 10 finish and valuable points in their overall UTWT ranking.

As long as you stay ahead of the camel, thanks to the generous cut-off times there's a very good chance you'll finish. But if you harbour any desire of doing well in the race, this is where things can go wrong. Staying on the edge of your physical limits all whilst trying not to get too dehydrated, get lost, penalised for being on a drip, forgetting to pick up water, littering and most importantly, looking after your feet... If you're able to do this for six days, pushing your body to the limit, you'll do brilliantly! If not, you'll be back again.

39 LAVAREDO ULTRA TRAIL

📍 Cortina, Italy   〰 Alpine   📶 5,850m   📅 June   🌐 www.ultratrail.it

DISTANCE

119k

HR	MIN	SEC
1 2	3 4	0 0

FASTEST TIME (KNOWN)

| 2 3 | 2 3 | 0 0 |

TOBIAS' FINISHING TIME

CUT-OFF: 30HRS

67% COMPLETION RATE

I've long held the view that if you're going to run silly distances, then you might as well do it somewhere beautiful. And it doesn't get much more beautiful than the Dolomites. The UNESCO World Heritage Site is a veritable playground of pinnacles, steeples, spires and towers all rolling onto a luscious green landscape that wouldn't be out of place in a *Lord of the Rings* novel.

The jewel in the crown is the Tre Cime di Lavaredo, three enormous peaks that sit on the border of the Italian provinces of South Tyrol and Belluno. The highest of the three, Cima Grande, is an agonising one metre shy of 3,000m. Unlike its big sister, the UTMB (see also page 188), the Lavaredo is whispered about like a secret too precious to share. Much easier to gain a place in, but no less impressive to have finished, The North Face Lavaredo Ultra Trail is the ultimate trail runners' destination race. However, being 119km long and with 5,850m of ascent, this is not a race for the faint of heart. Indeed, if those figures make you want to sit down, grab a drink and put on your compression tights, then I'd suggest you opt for the slightly gentler 47km-long Cortina Trail, which, with 2,650m of ascent, is still not to be sniffed at. Or if you want a great view of the entire Ampezzo Valley, then the 20km Cortina Skyrace might be more your thing.

Most people will run through the night twice.

However, if you've got any form of running FOMO (Fear of Missing Out), then you'll be standing at 11 p.m. underneath the clock tower along the Corso Italia in the upmarket ski resort of Cortina d'Ampezzo amongst the glow of hundreds of head torches, ready for a long slog through the night. The atmosphere of any ultra marathon that starts at night is one of excitement mixed with trepidation and the Lavaredo is no different.

Although the race takes place at the end of June when the weather is much better, being in the mountains there is still a risk of snow blocking the paths on the sections above the snow line (of which there are many), dense fog or thunderstorms. Besides being a qualifier for the Western States 100 and offering four points for the UTMB, it's also part of the Ultra-Trail World Tour and attracts some of the biggest names in ultra-running, from Rory Bosio (two-time winner of the UTMB) to bare-chested trail running legend Anton Krupicka.

Runners have 30 hours in which to return back to Cortina – where the race starts and finishes.

Running through the mountains at dawn –
a cold but incredible experience.

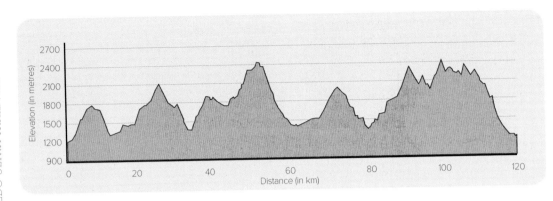

It's easy to see why participants unanimously agree this is one of
the most beautiful races on the European calendar.

Although the time limit of 30 hours sounds generous for 119km, when you factor in the technicality of the course and the crippling ascent and descent, it's not. This is one tough race. Similar to other ultra-marathons of this distance, your first mental hurdle will be reaching the theoretical halfway point, in this case at Rifugio Auronzo (48km into the race), where you'll have access to your drop bag – a potential source of morale, should you wish to change socks or restock on food. Of course,

with eight food and drink stops along the route, you'll have plenty of other opportunities to stock up. Hopefully, by this point night will have turned to day and you'll be starting to appreciate your surroundings. Enchanted woods, crystal blue lakes, snow-capped peaks, Avataresque waterfalls dripping off the mountains, World War I remains ... sometimes it's just too much to take in and you'll be wishing you had a camera.

In any event of this nature, where it's as much a journey as a competitive race, it's one you'll want to share. And although I travelled alone, I finished the race with a grin on my face, newly acquired friends and a warm reception from the Cortina locals who line the street to welcome you back. Which is of course what ultra-running is all about. Unless you're racing to the podium, for the mere mortals amongst us it's a chance to soak up the atmosphere, swap gasps and grunts with your fellow runners and simply revel in the moment. Because this is one race you'll never forget.

TOP: A runner making his way towards the 2,236m-high Giau Pass – where he'll be rewarded with spectacular views of the Ampezzo basin.

LEFT: Anton Krupicka winning the 2014 Lavaredo Ultra.

Top tips

- Take a camera or smartphone — the route is stunning
- Wear trail shoes with some cushioning and decent grip
- Walking poles will make your life much easier

ULTRA-TRAIL DU MONT-BLANC

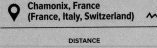

📍 **Chamonix, France**
(France, Italy, Switzerland) 〰〰 **Alpine – rain, snow and sun** 🪜 **10,000m**

📅 **August**

🌐 **www.ultratrailmb.com**

DISTANCE

170k

HR	MIN	SEC

2 0 1 1 0 0
FASTEST TIME (KNOWN)

3 1 3 4 5 2
TOBIAS' FINISHING TIME

CUT-OFF: 46HRS

60% COMPLETION RATE

It's 5.30 on a Friday evening and I'm standing beside a church in the centre of Chamonix, listening to Vangelis' 'Conquest of Paradise' playing on loud speakers. Bathing in the sun, which is casting an eerie glow onto the snow-capped Mont Blanc, looming above us like an ever-present friend, for a few blissful moments I almost forget about the enormity of the task ahead. Or the fact that the sun would settle

and rise several more times before I could rest. Suddenly there's a crack of a gun and I snap out of my moment of mindfulness to be carried forth in a virtual Mexican wave of arms, legs and poles: the race had begun.

Our task was simple: to run 105 miles around Western Europe's highest mountain and return to Chamonix within 46 hours. But as I cast a glance at some of the faces of my

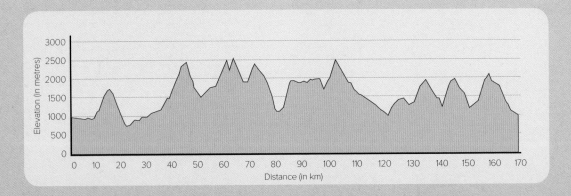

fellow ultra-runners trotting beside me, I had to remind myself that as many as half of us wouldn't finish.

Over the course of around 100 miles, you'll climb more than the height of Everest.

The Ultra-Trail du Mont-Blanc (UTMB) is the Grand National of ultra-running in Europe, if not the world. Elite and amateur ultra-runners gather to battle it out on Europe's most iconic hiking route: the Tour du Mont Blanc (GR5). Where most hikers aim to complete the trail in about 10–12 days, the winner will return to Chamonix after 20 hours. The speed at which they run is mind-boggling. As in fact is the entry process – just getting to the start line is an achievement in itself. Despite 2,300 places being made available, it's vastly oversubscribed. Consequently, some years ago the race organisers introduced an entry ballot combined with a points system to ensure that only those runners with sufficient experience are allowed to apply, even if they have no guarantee of being accepted. As of writing, you need nine points

divided between a maximum of three races completed within the preceding two years.

The route consists of 10 principal climbs, which will very much define how you break up the race. Most of them are runable with a few technical ascents/descents to keep you on your toes but hopefully not flat on your face. Which of course might well happen.

The main premise of the UTMB is built upon self-sufficiency and the capacity to be autonomous between the refreshment posts – which means you should not only be able to keep yourself fed and hydrated, but if the weather should turn foul or you should incur an injury, you should also be in a position to deal with it. Consequently, there is a rather exhaustive list of mandatory items that you need to bring with you, from waterproofs to a

ABOVE AND RIGHT: There's never a moment in the UTMB where you're not presented with a magnificent view!

LEFT: If the weather is unnaturally good, the crystal blue lakes you'll pass are a welcome distraction.

RIGHT: Some argue that the Italian stage of the UTMB is the most beautiful.

OPPOSITE: Arriving back in Chamonix 31 hours and 34 minutes after leaving it the previous day.

Top tips

- Print out the course profile so you know where the climbs/descents are
- Create a realistic schedule of when you need to reach the checkpoints
- Running poles are a godsend

survival blanket. And with spot checks along the course, you won't want to be without them. Luckily, the aid stations are a sight to behold. With 2,300 runners to feed and almost as many volunteers on the course, there is no end of food and drink to choose from, from bread and hot soup to cheese, biscuits, cake and fruit. At the business end of the field you'll have the place to yourself but as you get further down, it becomes busier than a kebab shop on a Friday night in London.

Although the winner will be home and dry by Saturday lunchtime, the average runner finishes somewhere between 35 hours and the 46-hour cut-off – which means that the majority of people will be running through the night not just once, but twice.

My initial goal was to finish within 28 hours, and therefore before night fell for a second time. My second goal was 30 hours – simply because that sounded like a good number. My third goal was before midnight. By the time I'd done 20 hours of running, my Achilles heel was screaming at me to stop and the first two goals went out the window. Ironically, I rolled into Chamonix weary but feeling a huge sense of achievement, in 31 hours 34 minutes – four minutes over my third goal!

41 BOB GRAHAM ROUND

📍 Keswick, Lake District, UK   〰〰 Fell   🪜 27,000ft   📅 An anytime challenge   🌐 www.bobgrahamclub.org.uk

DISTANCE

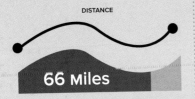

66 Miles

HR	MIN	SEC
1 3	5 3	0 0

FASTEST TIME (KNOWN)

0 0 0 D N F

TOBIAS' FINISHING TIME (DID NOT FINISH)

CUT-OFF: 24HRS

30% COMPLETION RATE

It's just before one o'clock in the morning on Saturday night and I'm standing alongside my running partner Adam outside Moot Hall in Keswick, holding onto its door handles whilst Adam's father takes a photo of us.

'Say cheese!'

I pathetically grin for the camera, trying not to blink as the flash goes off. Not far away, a group of friends are gathering around a runner, tired beyond comprehension. Some of her friends are holding fish and chips, others cans of beer. They were celebrating her rite of passage into the most exclusive running club in Great Britain – the Bob Graham Round Club.

Generally speaking, I always have a pretty good idea if I'm going to finish a race or not (unlike the Red Bull Steeplechase, page 142). However, considering only one in three are successful in completing the Round, the odds weren't in our favour.

A few minutes later, with only a few revellers to witness our departure, we set our watches and started running through the night, head torches on, the beams bouncing off reflective surfaces as we headed towards the looming peak of Skiddaw – our first of 42.

But the Bob Graham Round isn't a race and nor does it pretend to be. There's no entry fee, no mandatory kit list, no prize money, no medal, no T-shirt. The reward is membership

The Bob Graham Round starts and finishes at Moot Hall in Keswick.

of a body of men and women whose number is less than those who've climbed Everest or swum the English Channel.

In order to qualify for the Bob Graham Round Club you need to summit 42 of the highest peaks in the Lake District whilst covering around 66 miles and 27,000 feet of climbing, all within 24 hours. And until that fateful weekend in July 2014, I had no idea just how difficult that would be!

Before attempting the Round, there are a few things 'sensible' people should think about. First, most people would never dream of attempting the Round without having done numerous recces of the route, which can be conveniently split up into five legs. This will allow you not only to learn the route and the best racing line but more importantly gives you an idea of what you're letting yourself in for.

Second, you'll have recruited friends and members of the Bob Graham Round Club to assist in your attempt. If you're really popular, you'll have one friend to be your navigator and another to be your mule, who will carry essential supplies like food, water or spare clothing. These people will swap over with fresh recruits, at the four points accessible to the road on the route.

Third, you'll have carefully studied the route, memorising as much of it as you can, learning where the contours go.

Fourth, you'll create a meticulous schedule that will tell you at what time you need to reach each of the 42 peaks. Just like a marathon, you need to realistically decide how quickly you can complete the round, allowing for a small buffer in case you're late.

Fifth, you'll need to register your attempt with the Bob Graham Round Club secretary and each peak needs to have a witness – which is why you need to do it with someone else.

And finally, you should choose a day in the year, generally speaking as close to the Summer Solstice as possible, thereby maximising the daylight hours, and giving you the best chance of decent weather. If it rains and there's poor visibility, you'll need to be a map-reading ninja or have a very good GPS. But as we discovered, there's no guarantee of good weather in the Lakes.

There's nothing flat about the Bob Graham Round!

What I hadn't appreciated, not being a fell runner, was quite how difficult it is to run on the terrain. There are no well-marked trails to follow; it's a case of taking the best line – whether that be over bog, heather, rock or fell. There's also one rather tricky bit between Scafell Pike and Scafell, an accident blackspot called Broad Stand. It's the closest you'll get to rock climbing on the Bob Graham Round and needs careful planning if you want to avoid being rescued by the Wasdale Mountain Rescue Team.

Sadly, by the time we reached Wasdale Head, the end of the third leg and 40 odd miles and 24 peaks, we were 90 minutes behind schedule. Poor visibility, low cloud and miserable weather meant we'd been moving too slowly – which meant that our chances of completing the round in less than 24 hours were reduced to none, so we called it a day.

Although we didn't finish the Round, I enjoyed every moment of the 17 hours we spent on the fells. The Lake District is perhaps the most stunning part of the UK and whether you do just one leg, walk the Round over several days, or smash it out in 24 hours, it's just a joy to be in the hills. And what was initially an attempt became a recce – so it's not all bad.

Top tips

- Recce the entire route with someone who knows the racing line
- Spend at least six months training for the event
- Be realistic with your schedule

Being somewhat off the beaten track, there is a great feeling of peace and quiet in these parts of the Lakes.

42 THREE PEAKS RACE

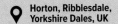 Horton, Ribblesdale, Yorkshire Dales, UK Fell 1,608m April www.threepeaksrace.org.uk

DISTANCE

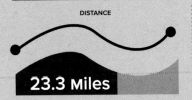

23.3 Miles

HR MIN SEC

0 2 4 6 0 0

FASTEST TIME (KNOWN)

0 4 2 5 0 0

TOBIAS' FINISHING TIME

87%
COMPLETION RATE

If ever I were to do just one fell race, then it might as well be the blue ribbon event of the fell-running calendar: The Three Peaks Race, also known as 'The Marathon with Mountains'. To avoid confusion, I'm not referring to the national Three Peaks Challenge which has become so popular of late. Nor am I talking about the Scottish Islands Peaks Race or the Three Peaks Yacht Race. Nope, I'm talking about the Yorkshire Three Peaks of Whernside, Ingleborough and Pen-y-Ghent.

Being one of the classic walks in the Yorkshire Dales, many people tackle the Three Peaks as a challenge, aiming to walk the circuit in less than 12 hours. But in the Three Peaks Race, the cut-off is around six hours – so by no means a walk in the park. In fact, in order to enter, you need to prove you have some fell-running experience or at least some decent marathon times.

Fell running is almost a sport unto itself, one that requires grit, stamina and an ability to navigate up hill and down dale. You only need to look at the photos of fell runners and you'll see the steely determination etched onto their faces as they brace the chilly climes of the north in nothing but a club singlet and skimpy pair of shorts. But fell running also involves a certain amount of self-sufficiency, and following 'severe weather conditions' in 1978, changes were made that required sufficient experience and certain mandatory items of kit. The idea being that if you come a cropper you need to be able to get yourself off the mountain. Which is why, as per the Fell Runners Association (FRA) rules, you need to carry a map (despite the course being marked), compass, whistle, hat, gloves, waterproof jacket and some 'emergency food'. Just in case.

The race dates back to 1954, where there were only six runners and three finishers. It became popular with fell runners all over the country, and then in 2008, it hosted the World Long Distance Mountain Running Championships, catapulting it onto the world stage. The premise of the race is simple: to run 23ish miles between the aforementioned Three Peaks and back again to Horton-in-Ribblesdale within the cut-offs, climbing around 1,600m in the process.

Runners making their way up towards the first peak of three –
the 694m high Pen-y-Ghent.

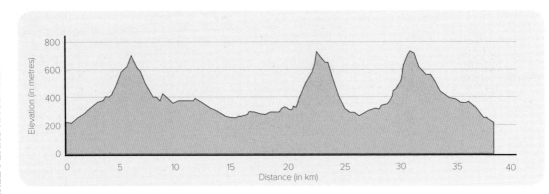

Moments away from reaching the summit of Pen-y-Ghent.

If you're hoping for a few easy miles to shake out your legs, think again. Within minutes of setting off, you're already at the foot of the first peak – the 694m high Pen-y-Ghent. And if you've not practised placing hands on knees before, you'll quickly get the hang of it. Reaching the summit after a good deal of huffing and puffing some 40 minutes later, I could see why they called this the 'Marathon with Mountains'. Compared to the Alps, the Three Peaks might be small, but they sure do pack a punch.

Having dibbed in (an electronic system of recording your time), I immediately scrambled off back in the direction I'd just come from, before

going on to the next peak – Whernside – possibly the most punishing of the three. With it being 10 miles away, along a series of rocky paths and boggy ground, this is a good time to get some food and water on board because you'll need it when you reach the monstrosity waiting for you.

After crossing a small but deceptively deep river near Ribblehead and then wading through a massive bog that saw many a person lose a shoe, you proceed to climb using both your hands and feet up the southern edge of Whernside. You arrive at the top only to be promptly blown off. It's definitely not a place you want to hang around.

Next up is Ingleborough, which strangely enough doesn't feel too bad. But maybe it's knowing that it's the final peak. But don't let this lull you into a false sense of security. The top is a rocky outcrop, similar to Scafell Pike, and here you will need the nimbleness of a squirrel to avoid twisting your ankle. But that's nothing compared to the strange geological limestone phenomena called Sulber Nick that will have you watch your footing with the attention of a hawk.

It takes a surprisingly long time to get back to Horton-in-Ribblesdale, and by the time I crossed the finish, some 4 hours 25 minutes later, I had a newfound respect for the world of fell running and the Three Peaks of Yorkshire!

Top tips

- Learn to descend on hills – a lot of time can be lost here
- Take on food and water between Pen-y-Ghent and Whernside
- Bring suitable clothing for the weather, not just the minimum required by the FRA

43

KILIAN'S CLASSIK

Font-Romeu,
Pyrenees, France  Mountain trail  1,700m+ July 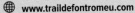 www.traildefontromeu.com

DISTANCE

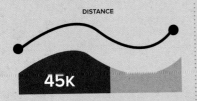

45K

HR	MIN	SEC
0 4	1 7	0 0

FASTEST TIME (KNOWN)

0 6	4 6	0 0

TOBIAS' FINISHING TIME

71%
COMPLETION
RATE

In the world of mountain and ultra-running, there is one name you'll hear a lot: Kilian Jornet. The Spanish ultra-runner and ski mountaineer has set multiple speed records up peaks such as the Matterhorn, Mont Blanc and Denali, along with Fastest Known Times on many of the toughest mountain trails in the world. He has also won almost all of the major mountain races across the globe, from the Western States 100 to Hardrock 100, making him arguably the king of the endurance world. So it's entirely fitting that a race should be named after the man who was born at altitude in the Spanish Pyrenees, giving rise to him becoming one of the greatest-living mountain athletes of all time.

Whilst the ski lifts sit empty, runners make their way towards one of the ski stations several thousand metres up.

Founded in 2011, the Kilian's Classik, or the Trail de Font-Romeu as it's also known, starts in the Eastern Pyrenean mountain town of Font-Romeu, a place famous for its skiing but perhaps less well known for its state-of-the-art altitude training centre, often frequented by Olympians Paula Radcliffe and Mo Farah amongst many others. It's also where Kilian discovered his love for mountain running.

But for this particular weekend, it's home to the Salomon International Team – who use the race as an opportunity to bring their elite athletes together in order for them to relax and enjoy running in the mountains without the pressure to perform. And for the 2,000 people who register for the race, it's a chance to meet and greet the rock stars of the ultra-running world, from Kilian Jornet and Emelie Forsberg to Anna Frost and Ryan Sandes. Luckily, the Salomon athletes start two minutes behind everyone else so it gave the rest of us mere mortals a chance to run with the stars, even if it was for only a few steps.

Although ultra-running purists might snigger at calling the 45km-long Kilian's Classic an ultra, with it being only three kilometres over a marathon, it's nevertheless a serious undertaking and being at altitude, it's a race that will take many of the competitors most of the day to complete. But if that all sounds a bit too much, there is always the shorter 25km option available. Regardless, the route, which passes through the two valleys of Grave and Carlit, has something to offer everyone, from stunning single track to technical scree running over shattered rock, some of which is so steep, I saw a number of people go down on their bottoms. Add to the mix the crystal-blue lakes, snow-capped peaks and mountain streams – it's impossible not to

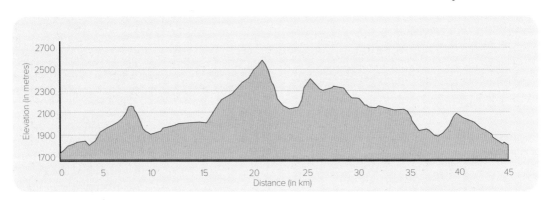

marvel at why the Pyrenees isn't inundated with trail runners more often.

With the entire race taking place at altitude, never going lower than 1,700m and rising to as high as 2,581m, like many others I spent much of the time gasping for breath as we slogged our way up near-vertical mountains, using the aid stations spaced every seven to eight kilometres to refuel and as an excuse to catch our breath. Some of the climbs were so severe, I had to pause halfway up to give my legs a rest.

Almost seven hours later (and two and a half hours behind Kilian), I arrived back in Font-Romeu, having totally reinvigorated my trail running mojo. I enjoyed a feeling of peace and tranquillity that I'd not often experienced in a race but perhaps that's the point. The Kilian's Classik isn't really a race, but a way of communicating one's passion for running in the mountains.

OPPOSITE: With the majority of the route being above 2,000m, it's not unusual to see snow – despite the race being held in July.

LEFT: A runner cautiously makes his way down a scree slope.

Top tips

- This is less of a race and more of a journey, so enjoy yourself
- Runnng poles could be useful as there are some long climbs

44 THE SANI STAGGER ENDURANCE RACE

📍 **South Africa**   〰 **Trail**   🏛 **1,600m**   📅 **November**   🌐 **www.sanistagger.com**

DISTANCE

26.2 Miles

HR	MIN	SEC
0 3	0 4	1 3

FASTEST TIME (KNOWN) MEN'S COURSE RECORD

| 0 4 | 4 6 | 0 0 |

TOBIAS' FINISHING TIME

71% COMPLETION RATE

On discovering that we'd be on holiday in South Africa in November at the same time as The Sani Stagger Race, one of the toughest and most iconic marathons in the country, I asked my wife Zayne if she'd like to do it with me. Generally speaking, any race that includes a few names like 'Haemorrhoid Hill' or 'Suicide Bend', or indeed 'Stagger', suggests either a misplaced sense of humour or possibly a warning to the uninitiated. The conversation went like this:

Me: So, can we do it?

Zayne: You know it's really, really hard, don't you? It runs along the Sani Pass, one of the most dangerous roads in Africa and has a fierce reputation for breaking people.

Me: Yeah, it goes up and then goes down. After all, it's only a marathon and it can't be any harder than the UTMB.

Zayne: OK, on your head be it! And don't tell me I didn't warn you. Anyway, since I'm the sensible person in the relationship, I'm going to enter the half.

Indeed, my wife might be right, because if you're contemplating a marathon high up in the Natal-Drakensberg Mountains that includes a gruelling 1,600m of ascent in the first 21km, before turning around and going back down the same hill, it might be wise to undertake a little specialised training.

Excellent though Clapham Common might be, or the Zig Zags of Box Hill, attempting an endurance race that's only run once a year and the rest of the time is tackled exclusively by 4x4s, donkeys and intrepid motor cyclists or mountain bikers is a challenge at the best of times. Cars are forbidden – they are not considered 'man enough' to get up the fiercely steep gradient. Nevertheless, since this iconic race organised by Sani Athletic Club was tucked away in my bucket list, I decided now was the time to give it a go – or at least try to, if I could get a place. The entries

The Sani Pass in all its glory.

open at 9 a.m. on 1 August and sell out the same day. With there being 230 half marathon entries and 500 for the marathon, there's clearly a lot of nutters in this world!

The race starts at Sani Pass Hotel and involves running across the golf course before reaching the track. Garbed only in my Clapham Chaser club running singlet and being a little tardy, foolishly I hadn't stopped to slather myself with sun cream lotion – a big mistake bearing in mind the race starts at 1,566m of altitude and the summit of the Pass is at 2,873m. I quickly discovered my shoulders didn't appreciate being so close to the African sun.

But that was nothing compared with the mere slog of getting up the mountain track. The average gradient is 1:20, but with over 1,000m of climbing in the second half, many sections are as steep as 1:4. As I passed the numerous hairpin bends, some aptly named Twin Streams, Ice Corner and Big Bend Corner, I could imagine that in a vehicle it would be hair-raising stuff. On foot, it's no better. By the time I'd reached the halfway point of 13.1 miles, to say I was not feeling my best would be an understatement. Sweating, dehydrated

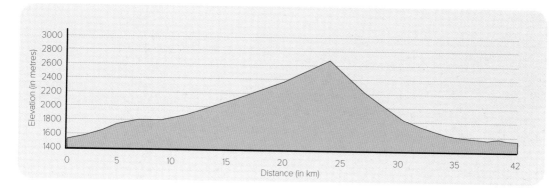

and cursing that I had not taken more notice of the fact that high altitude combined with the African sun would wreak its own particular toll on a runner, I was not a happy bunny.

Happily, when I eventually reached the top, two and a half hours later and almost a gibbering wreck, I caught sight of Zayne just starting the half marathon (she ran pretty much the whole of her race with me and would have done well if she hadn't been running with me). Luckily, the summit and entrance to the Kingdom of Lesotho were only a few hundred metres away. Sadly, having not brought my passport, I couldn't take advantage of the highest pub in South Africa, just across the border. I had no choice but to run feebly around the lonely-looking traffic cone and make my way back down.

By this time my legs resembled bags of jelly and if anyone considers the way up a tough call, the way down has its own treacherous and sneaky ways. Sliding stones and rough terrain require a level of concentration not easy to achieve when you feel you've already thrown everything at the mountainside and your quads are on fire.

I cannot, in all honesty, say this was my finest hour, but in every runner's life there comes a moment when you have to sacrifice pride and sheer bloody-mindedness. I confess that the Sani Stagger was probably my worst ever PB – with a very long, drawn-out 4 hours and 46 minutes. But it was also one of the most beautiful, stunning and extraordinary marathons I've ever done. As I crossed the finish line, back where I'd started, I was very happy to receive the finishers' medal, one that I'm very proud of – although, if I ever do it again, I'll put in more than a few runs up Box Hill!

Top tips

- Trail shoes aren't necessary unless it rains
- If you are not a South Africa resident, you'll need a temporary race licence (R35). The only runners who need passports are those doing the half because it starts at the top of the mountain and there's the option of going into Lesotho. The full marathon stops short of the border
- Add at least an hour and a half to your marathon PB to work out your estimated finish time

Although prettier, the descent is a killer on the quads.

HARD AS NAILS

LAKES IN A DAY
ULTRA RUN

45

📍 Lake District, UK   〰 Trail and fell running   📶 4,000m   📅 October   🌐 www.lakesinaday.co.uk

DISTANCE

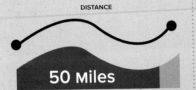

50 Miles

HR	MIN	SEC
1 0	3 7	0 0

FASTEST TIME (KNOWN)

| 1 3 | 3 1 | 0 6 |

TOBIAS' FINISHING TIME

89%
COMPLETION
RATE

One of the delights of running in the hills, that is when you're not falling into bogs, squelching about in mud, splashing through streams and scrambling up vertical hills, is the scenery. Of course, it's true that in a race you rarely have time to stand and stare at the beauty around you, though if you happen to be running the Lakes in a Day, the temptation is almost overwhelming.

When I first heard about this inaugural race organised by Open Adventure, I couldn't wait to sign up. Especially because this was no ordinary 'round' or 'east to west' route, but one that takes you all the way from the top of the Lake District at Caldbeck to finish at the bottom in Cartmel. Moreover, you have a whole 24 hours to cover some 50 miles and a cheeky 4,000m of elevation. This means you can either go for broke and cover it at breakneck speed (breakneck being at times an operative word) – or go for a more relaxed mode and take time to sniff the air and enjoy the glorious scenes that are all around you – as long as you make the cut-offs at the three aid stations! However, I've failed to mention two important points that separate this race from the many others on offer: the Lakes in a Day is a mash-up of fell running and trail running. What's more, you have to be self-sufficient and competent with a map and compass – something that will either appeal to your sense of adventure, or put you off.

OPPOSITE: At times, the trail skirts the shores of Lake Windermere.

ABOVE: As is typical of many fell races, there are lots of places where there are no marked trails.

Setting off from the village of Caldbeck, the first section takes you over the rarely visited Caldbeck Fells or 'Back O'Skidda', as the locals refer to it, which is often missed out by visitors in favour of the honeypot peaks in the fells to the south. But they lead you on to the difficult terrain of Mungrisdale Common – familiar to anyone who's attempted the infamous Bob Graham Round (see also page 194).

One of the tricky bits – and there are certainly more than one – is the descent from Blencathra. There's more than one route down and the most feared takes you directly into Hall's Fell Ridge, itself a fairly horrendous

Grade I scramble. It is also incredibly difficult to find the correct route. Come off the ridge too early and you'll be in a world of boulders, crags and technical terrain. Alas, I did take the wrong – and toughest – route and was followed by a group of runners, mistakenly thinking I knew exactly what I was doing! I wouldn't say I was popular as a result of my somewhat hazy map and compass reading.

In this race, navigational skills are important and whilst usually I am not too far off the mark, in this instance I must have been having a bit of a doze! However, as you slog your way up Clough Head and on to the Eastern Fells,

When the scenery is this beautiful, how can you not be smiling?

Top tips

- Familiarise yourself with the route
- Take a decent head torch (and spare batteries or a spare torch) if you think you're going to be going well into the night
- Consider a change of shoes at Ambleside

the fells and the beginning of the trail running section. After a quick refuel and change of shoes, I continued on my journey through the Lakes, following the shore of Windermere, England's longest lake, before reaching the final food station near Newby Bridge, just as day turned to night. After another quick bite to eat, I joined forces with several other runners, donning our head torches before heading south, comforted by the knowledge that it wasn't far to the finish.

Night running heightens your senses, making you so much more aware of your surroundings. It also makes it difficult to navigate and I had to concentrate on my bearings. Luckily, they were true, and after just over 13 and a half hours of running, I arrived in Cartmel, my journey across the Lake District complete.

The Lakes in a Day is a race that has a lot to offer – you can tailor it to your own level of fitness and experience and challenge yourself with night running, hardcore fell running, scrambling, peaceful trail running, skills with map and compass – or simply regard it as an exciting and pleasurable way to spend 24 hours. Whichever flicks your switch, this is without doubt one of the best ways to see the Lake District in all its glory.

navigation definitely becomes easier as you have the lovely ridge lines of Helvellyn to keep you on the right path. Of course, when the clouds come down and visibility is poor, trying to find minuscule footpaths in the gloom makes things much more difficult. But that's part of the joy of fell running. Being away from the masses, the world at your feet, and with no set paths to follow, the majesty of the mountains, your survival instincts kick in, making you feel incredibly alive, yet simultaneously free.

But of course, not everyone is so happy in the fells, and for many, reaching Ambleside was a welcome reprieve, as this signified the end of

46 ÖTILLÖ

From Sandhamn
to Utö, Sweden

〰 Trail and open-water swimming

📅 September

🌐 www.otillo.se

DISTANCE

75K
(INCLUDING 10K OF SWIMMING)

HR	MIN	SEC
0 8	1 6	0 0

FASTEST TIME (KNOWN)

1 2 4 3 2 5

TOBIAS' FINISHING TIME

81%
COMPLETION
RATE

Why, you might ask, if you're a keen trail runner, would you decide to complicate your life by going to Sweden to race across 26 islands of the Stockholm Archipelago? A race, moreover, that is 75km long but just to add to the fun requires you to swim 10km of those 75 in your wetsuit and sodden shoes! And that's not all: you have to be a two-person team, never more than 5m apart.

You might say the madness continued a further step, when I undertook the race, deemed to be one of the toughest one-day endurance races in the world, a week before my wedding.

'An excellent chance to bond,' I declared, as my chosen teammate was indeed my future wife, Zayne.

Now in its tenth edition, the ÖTILLÖ Swimrun World Championships attracts a wide range of individuals and demands that its entrants have a pedigree that includes a fair smattering of high-octane Ironman,

As the sun begins to set, teams of runners make the final dash towards the finish.

ultra-marathons and tough adventure races. And with only 120 team places available, getting one is a challenge in itself.

Although the terrain is varied, it's always beautiful.

Once you've celebrated your good fortune, you then have a second moment of deliberation when you realise this is a race that demands more than the usual amount of training. Especially if, like yours truly, water is not your most favourite habitat and your swimming skills, according to your future wife, give a whole new meaning to 'Doing the crawl'. Fortunately, aware I was the lesser swimmer, I took lessons, which stood me in good stead. However, you must be prepared for a number of things that do not ordinarily arise in a runner's life.

1. Take pleasure in soaking wet trainers – it's better than going barefoot over sharp rocks, along forest trails or animal tracks on uninhabited islands. But buy those that are as lightweight as possible and which drain freely.

2. Mad though it might seem, it's wise to drastically shorten the arms and legs on your wetsuit. It makes it cooler when you're running.

3. You may or may not want hand paddles – this depends on your swimming skills.

After joining the other competitors on the ferry journey from Stockholm to the island of Sandhamn, the start of the race, there was no time to waste in registering and discovering the all-important temperature of the water – something that had constantly preoccupied us in the build-up to the great day. With the race being the first Monday in September, the water can range from a very chilly 10°C to, by comparison, a balmy 16°.

Something else that was praying on our minds was the cut-offs. And with 50 transitions, it's easy to lose time faffing about as you put on

or remove hat, goggles, flotation device and hand paddles. Indeed, it is the fact that that apart from the mandatory equipment that includes a first aid bandage, wetsuit, compass, waterproof map holder, whistle and a bag to carry the equipment, everything else is optional, including a water bladder for hydration. If swimming isn't one of your strengths, then a flotation device and hand paddles will become pretty useful. But having a float in between your legs and the equivalent of flippers on your hands is not conducive to getting out of the water or running! However, after a mass run from the start, all our concerns disappeared the moment we entered the water for the first and longest of the 26 swims. 'Just keep moving, no matter what' was our motto for the day.

Strangely enough, despite the water being around 11°, it wasn't nearly as cold as we had imagined, though we did get the odd brain freeze. We quickly found a rhythm, keeping eye contact all the time lest we lose each other in the melee of similar-looking wetsuit-clad swimmers.

Finally reaching the first island, we had to practically roll ourselves up the slippery rock. Not the dignified look with which I'd wanted to impress my wife-to-be. But once on dry land, we were in our comfort zone and despite being last out of the water, quickly caught up with people who weren't so sure-footed.

There is one swim that everyone fears – the dreaded Pig Swim, so-named because it's quite

TOP: Early on in the race, it's common to see many other teams — a reminder you're not alone.

CENTRE: Most teams opt to carry some form of buoyancy aid which they wrap around their thigh or waist.

BOTTOM: Due to the slippery rocks, the hardest bit is often getting out of the water .

Top tips

- Ensure you and your teammate share the same goals and if possible, the same strengths

- Practise, practise, practise your transitions! Valuable time can be lost if you don't get the correct order of putting on hat, goggles, flotation device and hand paddles

- Do one of the ÖTILLÖ qualifier races. They're not only a great practice run, but also offer an opportunity to test out all your kit

Exhausted but happy, Zayne and I arrive at the finish.

simply a pig of a swim. An open channel of water, the 1,400m swim becomes longer due to aiming off for the current. By this stage my shoulders were aching from using hand paddles, which in the end I ditched, shoving them up the legs of my wetsuit. But having conquered the Pig, we simply had to run a half marathon and we'd reach the final checkpoint which closed at 18:00 hours on the island of Ornö. After that we could, within reason, take as long as we wanted to cross the five remaining islands.

Arriving at the finish line in Utö, we both felt an enormous sense of relief. The perfect blend of strength, stamina, teamwork and compassion, it's the race I'm most proud of finishing.

HARD AS NAILS

ECOTRAIL DE PARIS

Paris, France   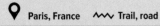 Trail, road   1,500m   March   www.traildeparis.com

DISTANCE

80K

	HR	MIN	SEC
	0 5	3 5	0 0

FASTEST TIME (KNOWN)

| 0 8 | 1 8 | 0 0 |

TOBIAS' FINISHING TIME

CUT-OFF: 13HRS

89%
COMPLETION
RATE

OPPOSITE: The start of the 80km race at St Quentin-en-Yvelines.

ABOVE: You'll pass many of Paris's most iconic buildings and monuments.

The EcoTrail de Paris is one of those races that immediately captures the imagination. The idea of running 80km of unadulterated trails through one of the most picturesque cities in the world is an attractive proposition in itself. But the grand finale is what really makes this race special: the finish line is on the first floor of the Eiffel Tower, after 328 steps of vertical ascent. Have I got your attention?

The premise of the race, as the name 'EcoTrail' suggests, is built upon ecology. As soon as you arrive at the start area in the Île de Loisirs at St Quentin-en-Yvelines, you're encouraged to think about the environment. In place of the customary portaloos, there are wooden drop short toilets within which you deposit handfuls of sawdust on your number two. There are bins everywhere, encouraging you to recycle your plastics. They even insist

you bring your own cup – in order not to waste plastic cups at the aid stations. And with 2,000 entrants, that's a big saving.

All of which was somewhat ironic, considering on the particular day I ran it in 2015, Paris was enveloped in a layer of smog so thick, they made public transport free to persuade people not to use their cars. We were probably the most environmentally friendly people in the whole of the city!

The main race starts at midday – which might seem a bit late in the day, but with the average finishing time being over 10 hours and with a 1 a.m. cut-off, this is designed so that the majority of people reach the finish at the Eiffel Tower by night. Indeed, many argue that thanks to the 20,000 bulbs that sparkle for five minutes on the hour, every hour, from dusk till 1 a.m., it's not until nightfall that you get to see the Tower in all its glory.

Much of the race follows trails through woods and parks.

It's said that that Paris in the springtime is at its most beautiful. Although the overcast weather (not to mention the aforementioned smog) wasn't helping matters on the day, it's impossible not to fall in love with this incredible city that has captured the hearts of so many. The run, of which 90 per cent is on paths, takes you through some of the most enchanting parts of Paris. Of course, it's also well known for its food, a fact you become very aware of at the aid stations. The French haven't quite grasped the concept of carbohydrates, preferring to stock you up with cheese, pepperoni and soup – a much more civilised alternative to energy drinks and gels.

The course has 1,500m of elevation – not an impressive figure on its own. But when you consider this spread amongst dozens of hills that fall into the 'short and sharp' category, 1,500m feels more than sufficient. There are a several points in the course when you catch sight of the finish appearing tantalisingly close, but thanks to the constant twists and turns, it soon becomes annoyingly far away. But eventually, as the evening draws in and day turns to night, the Eiffel Tower becomes an illuminated beacon of hope. Running the final section along the River Seine, it draws you in like a moth to the flame

Upon reaching the Tower, it's impossible not to feel in awe of its size. Stretching above you like a giant, one is suddenly grateful that the

Top tips

- Allow plenty of time to get to the start. It's a surprisingly long way out to St Quentin-en-Yvelines

- Take a camera or a smartphone

- Regular road running shoes are fine, but if there's even a hint of rain, then you'll want comfortable trail shoes

finish line isn't any higher than the first floor. After passing through security, a mere 328 steps remain between you and the finish. With the knowledge that the pain would stop in a few minutes' time, I bounded up them two at a time, even overtaking a few startled runners in the process, before crossing the finish line in 8 hours 18 minutes.

Strolling around the perimeter of the Tower, gazing at the lights of Paris sprawled beneath me, I couldn't think of a more appropriate way to earn my view.

So close, yet so far: The race finishes at the Eiffel Tower — which looks teasingly close yet can still be 20 miles away.

48 MADEIRA ISLAND ULTRA TRAIL

📍 Full traverse of Madeira Island   〰 Trail/mountain   🪜 6,800m   📅 April   🌐 www.madeiraultratrail.com

DISTANCE

115k

HR	MIN	SEC
14	36	00

FASTEST TIME (KNOWN)

22	27	00

TOBIAS' FINISHING TIME

CUT-OFF: 32HRS

74% COMPLETION RATE

'Have you heard of the Madeira Island Ultra Trail?' my wife Zayne asks me one Christmas, glancing up from a copy of a running magazine.

A few moments later we were huddled over my laptop, watching a video of a race that took runners through a land reminiscent of Arthur Conan Doyle's *The Lost World*. Soaring mountains hidden by mist, lush green foliage,

OPPOSITE: Although much of the race follows the famous 'lavados', some parts of the course are on stunning single track.

irrigation canals (known in Madeira as *lavados*) taking precious water from high in the mountain down to the drier sections near the coast, tunnels cut into the rock … it was other-worldly. It was also listed as a 'Future race' on the Ultra-Trail World Tour.

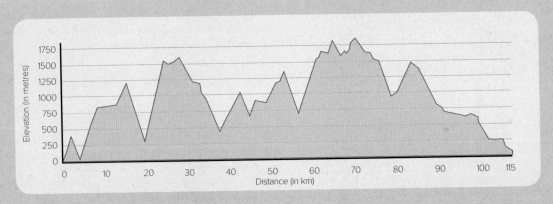

With four races on offer, the Madeira Island Ultra Trail (MIUT) has something for everyone: from a relatively tame 17K right through to the 115K blue ribbon event, and with a 40K and 85K option in between. Keen to see as much of the island as possible, I chose the main event, which manages to cram in an eye-watering 6,800m of ascent into 115km. The race does a full traverse of the island, starting in the northwest at Porto Moniz and finishing at the Fórum Machico. And like so many races of this distance, it starts at midnight – which means that if you finish at the 32-hour cut-off, you'll have been awake for the best part of 48 hours – enough time for anyone to turn into a walking corpse.

Although the race takes place in April, the weather in the mountains can be quite unpredictable. On the coast it can be hot and sunny, but above a certain altitude, the climate is in the lap of the gods – but the temperatures generally speaking are a good few degrees lower.

It's easy to see why Madeira is referred to as the Pearl of the Atlantic.

With 6,800m of ascent ahead no time was wasted from the get-go, with us immediately scrambling up a lung-busting hill on a road out of Porto Moniz. Once at the top, we descended a treacherous set of steps that most of the Portuguese runners flew down with effortless dexterity. It was only once at the bottom that I looked back to see an amazing zig-zag of torches cascading down the mountain side.

The night passed relatively quickly, probably because I was concentrating so hard on trying not to fall over. Apart from running beside the lavados, the terrain was incredibly technical: treacherous wooden steps that would be easy to trip over, slippery roots, randomly placed rocks – anything that made running difficult. Being reasonably strong on the hills, I'd make time on the ascents, only to lose it again on the way down, as I irritatingly watched everyone I'd just passed fly by me again.

In the first six hours of the race I'd covered the best part of 40km and almost 3,000m of climbing, but I wasn't even halfway. Not even close. Just at the point when I was starting to get weary and losing the will to run, the sun

OPPOSITE: The eventual winner, Luis Fernandes, making his way towards the beautiful Pico do Arieiro – the highest point of the course.

BELOW: With the race beginning at midnight, you'll want a decent head torch to see where you're going.

popped its head over the mountains, casting a warming glow not only on the rocks, but most importantly, on my body. Moreover, having had my blindfold of darkness removed, I could begin to appreciate the stunning scenery.

The landscape changed dramatically from the dense and tropical type of foliage to rough paths hewn out of the rock face that sometimes lead us into deep tunnels so dark the light from the other end was the size of a pinprick, forcing me to turn my head torch back on again. The highlight of the course was without doubt the 1,818m high Pico do Arieiro, the third highest peak on the island. The enormous jagged spires of rock with a blanket of cloud beneath, occasionally blown away by the wind, revealed panoramic views of the landscape around us. I could see why it's the

island's most visited tourist attraction. If ever a place could be called Eden, it would be the Pico do Arieiro.

I could hear the tannoy of the finish long before I saw it – although the winner had come through some eight hours earlier. By the time I crossed the line, it was almost 10.30 at night. The MIUT was everything I'd hoped for, and more.

Top tips

- Take walking poles – you'll need them!
- A wind cheater is especially useful at night, as it can get cold on the tops of the mountains
- At night the ground is treacherous, so take the most powerful torch you have

49 TRANSVULCANIA

📍 La Palma,
Canary Islands　　〰 Trail　　🪜 4,191m　　📅 May　　🌐 www.transvulcania.com

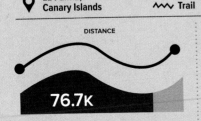

DISTANCE

76.7K

HR　MIN　SEC

0 6 : 5 2 : 0 0

FASTEST TIME (KNOWN) COURSE RECORD

1 : 3 5 : 5 1 3

TOBIAS' FINISHING TIME

CUT-OFF: 16HRS

60%
COMPLETION
RATE

That moment when you start to become delirious is a strange feeling. The heat is pounding down on you so hard you desperately search for even the tiniest bit of shade – anything that might help to cool you down. Although I'd already done about half a dozen 'ice bucket challenges' in the previous five hours, I was fast discovering that running up a volcano is hard work. It's the main reason why the 76.7km long Transvulcania is regarded as one of the toughest and most prestigious mountain races, not only in Europe but in the world too.

Over 10 million people visit the Canary Islands every year, but of that number only 300,000 will make it to the small island of La Palma, home to this land of volcanoes and the GR130 and 131, the two trails that provide the inspiration for this incredible race.

Although Transvulcania has been running since 2007, it's only since 2012, when it became part of the Skyrunning World Series, that it suddenly became a rock star in the ultra-running world. Attracting the best mountain runners in the world, from Kilian Jornet and Dakota Jones to Anna Frost and Emelie Forsberg, it's a chance for mere mortals to run with the gods high above the clouds in the National Park of La Caldera de Taburiente.

Starting at sea level, the race begins at 6 a.m. at the Faro de Fuencaliente, a prominent lighthouse in the south of the island. At 24m high, it looks proudly out to sea, warning ships of the dangerous rocks. But as we gathered beneath its watchful gaze, all eyes were looking inland.

Ask anyone about the start of the Transvulcania and you'll be met with a barrage of words, consisting of 'madness' or 'chaos'. Within minutes of setting off, and still dark at 6 a.m., almost 2,000 runners immediately converge on a narrow path leading them up a steep climb at the base of the two volcanoes of Teneguia and San Antonio.

Keen to avoid the 'madness' I opted to start near the rear, a decision that probably cost me 30 minutes but prevented me from going off too hard at the start. Some people tried to take shortcuts by coming off the path, but the ground is littered with razor-sharp rocks which, like booby traps, will rapidly bring to a halt any reckless runners.

Even though it was early as we passed through the town of Los Canarios, our first water stop, everyone was up to welcome us, or so it seemed. The generous and warm hospitality of the people of this island shines out whatever the hour. However, my relaxed approach meant that I reached the five-hour cut-off at El Pilar, a mere 24km away, with only 45 minutes to spare. I'd totally underestimated how long it would take to climb 2,000m – which, when condensed into a half marathon on technical terrain, turns out to be a lot harder than I'd imagined.

Alongside a head torch, a red rear light, a thermal blanket and a mobile phone, one of the key mandatory items of equipment is a hydration system capable of carrying at least one litre of water. As I plodded up the Roque de los Muchachos, which at 2,421m above sea level is the highest point on the island, I was so thirsty I didn't have enough saliva to lick a postage stamp! Having almost run out of water on a long stretch between two aid stations, I vowed that should I do the race again, I'd bring more water.

The course is shaped like a giant question mark built around the Taburiente Crater, meaning you're constantly able to see the finish, even though it never seems to be getting any closer. But the views were to die for. Beneath us, a blanket of cloud hid the sea, but in the distance it was possible to make out the neighbouring islands of Tenerife and La Gomera, their own volcanoes peeking above the clouds.

As the saying goes, what goes up must come down. The crippling 2,000m descent of Los Muchachos towards Puerto de Tazacorte is one of the most unpleasant I've ever experienced. One wrong foot, and you'll find yourself planting face first into razor-sharp volcanic rock – I hadn't concentrated so long and hard since taking my driving test!

But don't think it's all over once you've reached sea level at Tazacorte. Although this may well mark the end of the GR131, the sting in the tail is yet to come when the organisers turn you around and make you finish 5km further uphill at the town of Los Llanos de Aridane. However tough the final few miles feel, every ache and pain evaporates the moment your feet touch the red carpet and pass under the finishers' archway when the full magnitude of what you've achieved hits you. And only then do you realise why this race is held in such high regard by the world's best mountain runners.

Top tips

- Take an extra half-litre of water. If you don't drink it, you can always pour it over your head!
- I didn't take walking poles, but I wish I had
- Don't make my mistake and wear black (it soaks up the sun) – go for light colours or white

Panoramic views can be admired on the way to the volcano's summit.

HARD AS NAILS
50 THE DRAGON'S BACK RACE

 From Conwy to Llandeilo, Wales 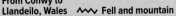 **Fell and mountain** **16,000m** 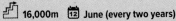 **June (every two years)** 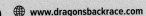 **www.dragonsbackrace.com**

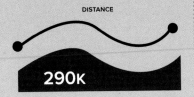

DISTANCE

290K

```
HR    MIN   SEC
4 0 | 0 8 | 0 0
```
FASTEST TIME (KNOWN)

```
6 1 | 2 1 | 0 0
```
TOBIAS' FINISHING TIME

50% COMPLETION RATE

I've saved this race until last for no other reason than because it represents the swansong of my journey in writing a book called *50 Races to Run Before You Die*. All the races in this book, the thousands of miles run and tens of thousands of metres climbed, all of them have been in preparation for the Dragon's Back Race – arguably one of the toughest mountain races in the world.

As I stood in the bowels of Conwy Castle, listening to the Maelgwn Male Voice Choir sing, I had to pinch myself. For over three years I'd waited for this moment, but it felt like a lifetime. I'd seen the photos from 1992, read numerous accounts of the race, watched the film of the 2012 event, and now, it was my turn.

The Dragon's Back Race is a five-day, 180-mile race across the mountainous spine of Wales, with accumulated climbing almost twice the height of Everest. But to understand the symbolic importance of the event, one must go back in time to 1992, when the first edition took place. With huge press coverage, TV crews and the like, it attracted the best athletes from around the world, including members of the Special Forces, a three-time Spartathlon winner and elite British mountain runners, to name but a few. Much to the surprise of many, a relatively

The race starts at the medieval Conway Castle.

The Pen-y-Pass YHA in the background, as runners scramble up Crib Goch.

unknown woman won the race – one Helene Diamantides (now Whitaker) with her running partner, Martin Stone. It was also the first time a woman had won an ultra-marathon outright.

To many a runner's dismay, the race didn't take place again for another 20 years. Originally organised by members of the Parachute Regiment, it was deemed not only too difficult a challenge to organise logistically, but also too hard to complete. In 1992, only a third of the competitors finished the race.

Twenty years later, with the race having been brought back from the dead by Shane Ohly, an experienced runner and event organiser, history repeated itself when at the end of Day 1, only

31 out of the 82 teams managed to finish the stage. By the end of the week, that number had reduced down to 29.

There are a number of factors that make the Dragon's Back Race challenging:

1. There is a massive emphasis on self-sufficiency. You need to carry sufficient equipment to survive in the mountains, from waterproofs and a bivvy bag through to water and food.

2. The course isn't marked. It's up to you to navigate your way from checkpoint to checkpoint, using nothing but your map and compass (and, if necessary, a little help from your GPS).

3. As a mountain race there are no defined trails; instead you're following sheep trods and contours.

4. There are strictly enforced cut-offs, meaning that should you make a navigational error, become lost, get injured or simply find you're not fit enough to make it through in time, then you're effectively out of the race, although you can continue in an unranked fashion.

With all these thoughts rattling around my head, I had one goal and that was to finish. My strategy was to take each checkpoint at a time, each day at a time, and not worry about anything else – a tactic that appeared to work.

On the first day, which was 49km long but with a crippling 3,800m of ascent, we tackled the majority of the Welsh 3000s, including vertigo-inducing Crib Goch and the brutal Snowdon Horseshoe. This was the stage I'd been worried about more than any other, being the most technical. Despite the poor visibility, the navigation was relatively easy, thanks to having recced this part of the route several weeks earlier.

But unlike many other multi-stage races, the camp at the Dragon's Back was the stuff of dreams. All the tents were set up for us, dinner was provided all evening, free massage, a medical tent to get patched up, if needed –

It might only be a Grade 1 scramble, but one false step on the knife edged 'arete' of Crib Goch and it's game over.

nothing was left wanting. Having dibbed in, one immediately fell into a routine of survival: eat, get a massage, stretch, fight midges, sort out kit for next day, sleep … Anything and everything that would help the body to recover. However, from the end of Day 1, I was in new territory. With a full day's worth of hills in the legs, Day 2 was challenging for various reasons. At 54km and 3,544m of ascent, it was a little longer and had slightly less climbing but traversed the formidable Moelwyns and Rhinogs. If ever there were two mountains I never wanted to see again, it was the two Rhinogs of Fawr and Fach. But it was the heat that really took its toll that day, with a number of runners suffering sunstroke. And although

the hills were slightly smaller, there were a lot more of them, making it a tough day for all.

Most people wouldn't choose to run 68km on their birthday, but if I wanted to get to the end of Day 3, the longest of all the stages and summiting the Cadair Idris and Plynlimon, I had no choice. For many, myself included, it was also the toughest day as the cumulative effect of running every day was taking its toll on our now-weary bodies. It also saw the largest number of withdrawals from the race, with another 19 dropping out, leaving only 56 per cent of those who started, still in: The Dragon was having its revenge.

With the longest stage out of the way, one would imagine Day 4 would be easy. And by comparison it was, although only fractionally

The treacherous Crib Goch proves testing on the legs.

Two hundred miles and five days later, I reached the finish at Carreg Cennen Castle in the Brecon Beacons. An amazing place to finish these 50 epic races.

shorter, at 64km but with a mere 2,273m of climbing. If ever there was a day to master the art of taking a bearing, this was it, especially when fighting your way through tussocks of purple moor-grass, bogs and anything else Elan Valley could throw your way. But this was in contrast to the 10km of road running that takes you to the final campsite.

The final day, 56km in length, took us over the Brecon Beacons – an area of Wales I knew well from my army days. So when the race director announced that there would be 30mp/h winds and heavy rain, I almost laughed out loud in disbelief. Sure enough, the weather forecast was accurate and we found ourselves running as fast as we could, hopefully in the right direction, in a vain attempt to simply stay warm and get to the end as quickly as possible.

By the time I reached the finish at Carreg Cennen Castle I'd been running a total of 61 hours 21 minutes. I'd used every trick in the book to keep myself going throughout the five days of running – not pushing it too hard, trying to take the best line possible, eating plenty of food, both on the hills and in the evenings, wearing compression leggings and elevating my legs. And now it was over, my body gave one last weary sigh, and relaxed.

It was done: I'd survived the Dragon. And now I could rightfully lay claim to being one of a very small number of people who have run the Dragon's Back! Thankfully, it's just the start of a whole new adventure.

ACKNOWLEDGEMENTS

Over the ten years of racing that this book encompasses, it would be fair to say it could take me almost as long to thank those who've helped me. Without doubt, a special thanks must go to the race directors, marshals and the fantastic volunteers who've tirelessly stood in the rain handing out cups of water, jelly babies or simply pointing me in the right direction. It should be said that without volunteers, none of these races would happen.

I also want to thank the numerous friends that I've met and worked with through running, too many to mention, but some too important not to: Bruce Duncan, James Thurlow, Matt Ward, Tord Nilson, Nick Gracie, Lee Procter, Andy Bruce, Wes Crutcher, Jay Goss, Fred Keeling, Shane Ohly, Simon & Julie Freeman, Damian Hall, Guy Jennings, James Heraty, Robbie Britton, Tim Hill, Adam Marcinowicz, Dan Whitney, James Carnegie, James Hendy and the ever-growing membership of my local running club, the Clapham Chasers.

There is one individual who deserves a special mention – my old friend Phil Davies. We've spent many an evening chatting about the races we'd like to do. It was his brilliant idea to enter the 2011 Marathon des Sables – a catalyst for the career I now have. Thanks mate!

Of course I should also mention that many of these races wouldn't have been possible without the support of the various brands who've kitted me out on my journalist endeavours over the years: Inov8, Salomon, adidas, adidas Eyewear, Asics, Merrell, Haglöfs, The North Face, SatMap and Black Diamond.

I'd also like to thank the editors of the magazines and newspapers that initially commissioned me to take part in these races, such as *Runners World*, *Men's Running*, *Men's Fitness*, *Outdoor Fitness* and *Telegraph Men*. And then there's the super talented photographers who captured the pain and glory of these races, bringing life to the pages of this book.

Special mention should go to Robin Harvie for commissioning me to write the book, to my editor Lucy Warburton and her team at Aurum Press for their tireless support and making the book look so fantastic. But above all, I should thank my mother for her inspiration and never flinching and belief in my abilities, both as a writer and as an athlete. And last, but not least, to my dear wife Zayne, for the never-ending pinks slips and accompanying me on so many of the adventures and races in this book.

PICTURE CREDITS

Disclaimer